# Is THIS LIFE all there is?

*Many common beliefs about life and death have held millions in the grip of fear. This book has been published in the hope that it will aid sincere persons to enjoy the freedom that only the truth can give. May it help you to find real purpose in living now and to have a grand hope for the future.*

*—The Publishers*

Publishers
WATCHTOWER BIBLE AND TRACT SOCIETY
OF NEW YORK, INC.
INTERNATIONAL BIBLE STUDENTS ASSOCIATION
Brooklyn, New York, U.S.A.

First Edition
2,500,000 Copies

Made in the United States of America

# CONTENTS

NOTE: Unless otherwise indicated, Bible quotations in this book are from the modern-language *New World Translation of the Holy Scriptures,* revised edition of 1971.

Will it ever be possible for man to live forever?
Some trees now live for many centuries.

## CHAPTER I

# You Have Reason to Be Concerned

IS LIFE precious to you? Do you desire life in good health for yourself and your loved ones? Most people will answer, Yes.

But today many things constantly remind us of the uncertainty of life—for ourselves, our mates and our children. Accidents, crimes, riots, wars and famines cut down millions right in the prime of life. Disease takes an appalling toll despite medical advances. Pollution poses a most serious threat.

It is not strange, then, that many persons today ask: 'Is this life all there is? Or can it be that our fondest hope is to be found in a life after death? What actually does happen when a person dies? Does some part of him live on? Is he still conscious, able to see, hear, talk—to do things? Is there such a thing as torment after death? Really, is death a friend or an enemy?' Surely it is to our benefit to know the answers to these questions.

## DOES DEATH MOLD OUR LIVES?

You may not have thought about it, but the lives of all of us are molded greatly by the view we hold of death. It affects our enjoyment of life and the way we use our lives far more than most people realize. That is why we need to know the truth about death.

Do you realize, for example, that most of the

world's religions are basically *death-oriented* rather than *life-oriented?* Hundreds of millions of persons have been taught that death will introduce them into another world, 'the world of the dead,' where they face either bliss or torment. Prayers for the dead, costly ceremonies on their behalf and sacrifices to appease them form a vital part of many major religions with vast memberships.

One may say: 'Perhaps so, but I don't spend my time worrying about death or what comes after it. My problem is living and getting as much as I can out of life now while I can.' Yet even that response shows death's molding effect on people's lives. After all, is it not death that determines how long it is before one can no longer get anything out of life?

So, even though we may try to blot the thought of death from our minds, the realization that our life-span is, at best, quite short keeps pressuring us. It may drive a person in a fierce effort to become rich at an early age—'while he can still enjoy things.' The shortness of life makes many people impatient, rude, callous toward others. It moves them to use dishonest ways to reach their goals. They just feel there is not time to do it the right way. Yet, all the while they may claim that death has no part in molding their lives.

What is your own view of death? What part does it play in your thoughts for the future, or, for that matter, the way you are living your life right now?

## THE NEED TO BE SURE

The problem is that there is such a wide variation among people's views about life and death.

Often the views are contradictory, exact opposites.

Many people believe that death is the complete end of everything or, at least, that man was made to die. Do you find that acceptable? Does it make sense to you that certain trees can outlive intelligent man by thousands of years? Do you feel that seventy or eighty years of life is long enough for you to do all that you want to do, to learn all that you want to learn, to see all that you want to see and to develop your talents and abilities to the extent you desire?

Then there is the tremendous number of persons who believe that life goes on after death because something—soul or spirit—survives the death of the body. Yet their views also differ greatly. And, of course, their beliefs contradict the idea of those who think that all life ends with death. Contradictory views cannot all be true. Which are right? Does it matter? Yes, very much. Consider why.

For one thing, if the dead can actually benefit from prayers and ceremonies on their behalf, would we not be merciless if we failed to provide these? But what if the dead are really dead, beyond the help of surviving humans? That would necessarily mean that hundreds of millions of persons are victims of a terrible fraud. It would mean that many great religious systems have enriched themselves by deceit, using falsehoods about the dead to exploit the living instead of doing something beneficial for them.

What comfort can we offer when, sooner or later, death invades our family circle, or that of a friend? Does logic support the view that "fate" governs our experiences and the length of our lives? What if the one dying was a small child?

Did God 'take the child to be with Him,' as some would say?

Truly there are many, many things we need to know about death, and the more we love life the more we should want to be sure to get the right answers. But where—especially since there is so much confusion and contradiction?

There are many religious books that discuss life and death, some of them quite ancient. But there is one very ancient book that presents a viewpoint quite different from that of all the others. In fact, the view it presents is surprisingly different from what the great majority of people think it contains. That book is the Bible.

It deals with real people, people who faced the same basic problems that we do today. They, too, pondered the whole purpose of living, asking: "What does a man come to have for all his hard work and for the striving of his heart with which he is working hard under the sun?" "Even supposing that he has lived a thousand years twice over and yet he has not seen what is good, is it not to just one place that everyone is going?" (Ecclesiastes 2:22; 6:6) They, too, raised the question: "If an able-bodied man dies can he live again?" (Job 14:14) Do you know the answers?

In the publication you now hold in your hands you will find discussed, not only the many popular attempts to answer the questions thus far raised, but also the vitally important way the Bible answers each of these. You can learn the unique hope it presents for those facing death or who have come within its grip. The understanding that this information can bring can contribute much to your present and future happiness and peace of mind.

## CHAPTER 2

# How Death Affects People's Daily Lives

MOST people are very much concerned about what affects their lives and that of their families right now. But few are willing to speak or to think extendedly about death.

True, death is not a bright prospect, but it has a definite effect on one's daily life. Who of us has not experienced the grief and deep sense of loss over the death of a dear friend or beloved relative? A death in a family can change the family's entire pattern of life, destroy a stable income and cause loneliness or depression for the survivors.

Unpleasant though it may be, death is a daily occurrence with which you must reckon. You cannot prolong certain actions indefinitely. Tomorrow may be too late.

How has this affected you? Do you at times feel pressured by the shortness of life to try desperately to get all that you can out of it? Or, do you take the fatalistic view, concluding that, well, what will be will be?

## THE FATALISTIC VIEW

Many people today believe that life and death are governed by fate. This is a basic concept of more than 477 million Hindus. In fact, fatalistic views are practically universal. Have you not heard people say, 'It just had to happen,' 'His time was up,' or, 'He escaped because his number wasn't up'? Such statements are frequently made in connection with accidents. Are they true? Consider an example:

During a demonstration flight at the Paris Air Show in 1973 the Soviet Union's supersonic airliner TU-144 exploded, killing its crew. Large sections of the aircraft hurtled down upon the village of Goussainville, France. One woman there had just shut the bedroom door behind her when a part of the wreckage came smashing through the outside wall, completely demolishing the bedroom. She was unharmed.

Others did not escape. The victims included an elderly woman's three grandchildren, but not the grandmother.

Did those children and others die because their "number" or their "time" was up? Were others spared because fate was not due to claim them until later?

Those answering "Yes" to these questions believe that nothing anyone might do can prevent a person's death if his 'time is up.' They feel that, despite any precaution taken, they simply cannot escape what fate dictates. This is a view similar to that of the ancient Greeks who considered man's destiny to be controlled by three goddesses —Clotho, Lachesis and Atropos. Clotho supposedly spun the thread of life, Lachesis determined its length and Atropos cut it off when the time was up.

Is such a fatalistic outlook reasonable? Ask yourself: Why do the number of accidental deaths decrease when safety regulations are obeyed and increase when they are disregarded? Why can the majority of traffic deaths be demonstrated to result from human carelessness, drunkenness, error or lawlessness? Why is it that in countries with high standards of hygiene and good diet people have a far greater average life-span than in countries lacking these things? Why do more smokers than nonsmokers die of lung cancer? How could all of this be due to blind fate over which there is no control? Instead, is it not the case that there are *reasons* for what happens to man?

With many accidental deaths, is it not a matter of a person's just happening to come into a dangerous situation? To illustrate: A man leaves his home at a certain time each workday. One morning, as he passes a neighbor's house, he hears screaming and shouting. He speeds up his walking and, just as he turns the corner, he is hit by a stray bullet. His death is due to his being at the

Does fate control your life, as the ancient Greeks believed?

corner at the wrong time; the circumstance was unforeseen.

Having observed what really happens in everyday life, the wise writer of the Bible book of Ecclesiastes said: "I returned to see under the sun that the swift do not have the race, nor the mighty ones the battle, nor do the wise also have the food, nor do the understanding ones also have the riches, nor do even those having knowledge have the favor; because *time and unforeseen occurrence befall them all*."—Ecclesiastes 9:11.

The person who appreciates this does not disregard safety regulations and take needless risks, thinking that he is immune to death as long as his "time" is not up. He realizes that a fatalistic view can be dangerous, both to himself and to others. This knowledge, wisely applied, can add years to your life.

On the other hand, a fatalistic outlook can lead to foolhardy actions, and it can also cause a person to be negligent about informing himself as to matters that may deeply affect him and his family.

### LIVING ONLY FOR THE PRESENT

Besides the fatalistic outlook, the events of the twentieth century have influenced people's actions.

Consider for a moment what has happened. Millions have perished as victims of war, crime, riots and famine. Life-sustaining air and water are being polluted at an alarming rate. Seemingly from every quarter man's life is being threatened. And there is nothing to give real assurance that mankind will be able to solve its problems in the near future. Life seems so uncertain. What is the result?

Many of earth's inhabitants are living only for the present, to get everything possible out of today. They feel impelled to do so, reasoning that the life they have now is all the life they can ever hope to have. Aptly the Bible describes their attitude: "Let us eat and drink, for tomorrow we are to die."—1 Corinthians 15:32.

In an endeavor to escape the harsh realities of life, they may turn to alcohol or drugs. Others try to find an outlet for their frustrations and concern over the shortness of life by personally indulging in sexual experiences of all kinds— fornication, adultery, homosexuality, lesbianism. Says the book *Death and Its Mysteries:*

> "It seems that more normal people today are affected by this fear of collective death, at least unconsciously. This is at least a partial explanation of the disarray of our times, which is expressed in gratuitous crime, vandalism, eroticism and the accelerated pace of life. Even modern music and dances seem to express the despair of a humanity that no longer believes in its own future."

What has been the effect of all such living for the present as if there may be no tomorrow?

Those given to heavy drinking and drunkenness may temporarily forget their troubles. But they sacrifice their dignity and, while intoxicated, at times injure themselves or others. And the next day they find that they have added an agonizing headache to the troubles that they already had.

Drug addicts, too, pay a high price for their efforts to escape reality. They often experience lasting physical and mental harm. And, to support their costly habit, they may find that they are degrading themselves by engaging in theft or prostitution.

What about promiscuous sex relations? Do they help to improve one's lot in life? To the contrary, the fruitage is frequently a loathsome venereal disease, unwanted pregnancies, illegitimate children, abortions, a broken home, bitter jealousy, fighting and even murder.

Of course, many persons have not succumbed to living a debauched life. Still they have not escaped the pressure that comes from realizing, consciously or subconsciously, that their life will end. Knowing that time is limited, they may seek to get ahead in the world just as quickly as possible. With what result? Their desire for material possessions may prompt them to sacrifice personal honesty. As the Bible proverb truthfully states: "He that is hastening to gain riches will not remain innocent." (Proverbs 28:20) But that is not all.

So much time and energy are used in getting ahead materially that there is little time to enjoy one's family. True, the children may be getting all the material things that they want. But are they getting the guidance and correction they need in order for them to become responsible young men and women? Many parents, while realizing that time spent with their children is somewhat limited, really see no reason for special concern—until it is too late. Yes, it is agonizing to learn that one's own son has been arrested or that one's own teen-age daughter is going to be an unwed mother.

From what is happening today, is it not obvious that, despite the shortness of life, many people need to learn a more satisfying way to live?

The apparent inevitability of death does not make everyone throw moral principles to the wind, nor does it produce a fatalistic apathy in all persons. To the contrary, hundreds of thousands today are enjoying a wholesome way of life because of not being adversely affected by the prospect of death.

## A BETTER WAY

Viewed aright, death can teach us something valuable. When death claims victims, we can benefit from thoughtful contemplation about the way we are living our own lives. Some three thousand years ago a careful observer of humanity highlighted this, saying: "A name is better than good oil, and the day of death than the day of one's being born. Better is it to go to the house of mourning than to go to the banquet house, because that is the end of all mankind; and the one alive should take it to his heart. . . . The heart of the wise ones is in the house of mourning, but the heart of the stupid ones is in the house of rejoicing."—Ecclesiastes 7:1-4.

The Bible is not here recommending sadness in preference to rejoicing. Rather, the reference is to the particular time when a household is in mourning over the death of one of its members. It is no time to forget the bereaved and to proceed with one's own feasting and reveling. For, just as death has ended all the plans and activities of the deceased, it can do the same for ours. A person does well to ask himself: What am I doing with my life? Am I building up a fine name or reputation? How much do I contribute to the happiness and well-being of others?

Not at birth, but during the full course of our

life, does our "name" take on real meaning, identifying us as to what kind of persons we are. The person whose heart is, as it were, in a "house of mourning" is one who gives heartfelt consideration to the way he is living his life, regardless of how short it may be. He treats it as something precious. He does not reflect the shallow, reckless spirit characteristic of a place of revelry. Rather, he exerts himself to lead a meaningful, purposeful life and thereby contributes to the happiness and welfare of fellowmen.

How can anyone determine whether he is now enjoying the best way of life possible for him, whether he is truly living a purposeful life? Certainly a standard of judgment is needed. In increasing numbers sincere persons throughout the earth are coming to the conclusion that the Bible is that reliable standard. Their examination of the Bible has enabled them to find real purpose in life now and it has given them a grand hope for the future, a hope that involves life under righteous conditions on this very earth. They have come to realize that, not death, but life is God's purpose for mankind.

## CHAPTER 3

# *Man Was Made to Live*

GOD made man to live. This is what the Bible indicates by its description of the provisions that God made for our first human parents, Adam and Eve. It informs us that Jehovah God placed them in a beautiful garden home, a paradise,

occupying a section of the region called "Eden."
That paradise contained everything needed for
them to continue living. Concerning this, Genesis,
the first book of the Bible, says: "Jehovah God
made to grow out of the ground every tree
desirable to one's sight and good for food and
also the tree of life in the middle of the garden
and the tree of the knowledge of good and bad."
—Genesis 2:9.

Note that there was, not a 'tree of death,' but
a "tree of life" in this lovely paradise. That "tree
of life" stood as an unchangeable guarantee of
continued life to those entitled to partake of it.
There was no reason for Adam and Eve to have
a morbid fear of the possibility of dying. As long
as they continued to be obedient to their Creator
in not eating of the forbidden "tree of the knowledge of good and bad" their life would not end.
—Genesis 2:16, 17.

But is what the Bible says about man's being
made to enjoy an endless life-span in agreement
with what we can see of life? Do not the facts
show that humans have been dying for thousands
of years? Yes, but did you know that right in
your own makeup is evidence suggesting that
you should have a far longer life-span than is
customary in our day?

Consider, for example, the human brain. Is it
designed for a lifetime of just seventy or eighty
years? Interestingly, biochemist Isaac Asimov,
in commenting on the brain's capacity, noted that
its filing system is "perfectly capable of handling
any load of learning and memory which the
human being is likely to put upon it—and a billion
times more than that quantity, too."

Is it logical for man's brain to have a storage capacity for information a thousand million times as great as he is able to use during what is today an average life-span? Rather, does this not indicate that man was made to live a lifetime that would require a brain with an infinite capacity for memory?

This is by no means all.

## MAN ALONE HAS A CONCEPT OF ETERNITY

A remarkable point to note here is that the Bible sets only before man—not before any of earth's other creatures—the prospect of limitless life. In fact, it says that even the concept of past or future time indefinite or eternity is unique to man. Noted the inspired writer of the Bible book of Ecclesiastes: "I have seen the occupation that God has given to the sons of mankind in which to be occupied. Everything he has made pretty in its time. Even time indefinite he has put in their heart."—Ecclesiastes 3:10, 11.

Now, if what the Bible says about man is true, we should be able to see evidence to this effect. Do we? Does man stand in sharp contrast with the animals? Does man alone think seriously about the future, concern himself with it and work toward it? Does he react to death in a way different from the animals, showing that he alone has appreciation for what life has meant to him in the past and could mean to him in the future?

There is no denying that all living things cling to life. Instinctively animals that are eaten by other animals seek to escape their predators by flight or concealment. Many creatures will struggle against what appear to be impossible odds to

protect their young from death. Rabbits have
been known to kick so violently as to send rac-
coons sprawling. In the western part of the United
States a female antelope was observed success-
fully defending her kid from a timber wolf, her
sharp hoofs injuring his hindquarters and knock-
ing out his teeth. As he was seeking to get away,
she jumped on top of him and trampled him to
death.

Such instinctive reaction to the threat of death
plays a vital role in the preservation of creature
life. But does this mean that animals have an
appreciation for the past and future as does man?

As we know, a man can reflect on the past and
can plan for the future. In the privacy of his own
home, he can think back to his boyhood days
—his pranks, disappointments, failures, successes
and joys. He can plan future moves—building a
new house, purchasing furniture, determining the
kind of education he would like for his children
to get, and so forth. But can a dog, for example,
meditate about its puppyhood, the children that
played with it then, its becoming full grown and
then mating? In his book *Animals Are Quite
Different,* Hans Bauer shows what research has
revealed:

> "The dog will always need an actual sense-
> impression to enable it to conjure up former inci-
> dents. He may be taken, let us say, on a certain
> occasion to an unfamiliar town in which he under-
> goes some experience or other. After his return home
> the impressions then received will have been forgot-
> ten. But if he goes back to the same spot he will
> remember them. It is in fact one of the special pe-
> culiarities and advantages of the human as compared
> with the animal psychological structure that the con-
> tent of human memory is not associated with the

needs of every day but embedded in the stream of consciousness as a whole."

Thus, unlike man, animals cannot at will reconstruct events of the past.

But can they plan ahead for the future? Do not hamsters, certain ants, squirrels and other animals store up or hide food supplies for later use? Is not this a planning ahead for the future so as not to suffer want in winter? "No," says the above-mentioned author, and he gives these facts in support:

"They do not know what they are doing or why they do it. They simply proceed in accordance with instinct, the proof being that even animals removed from their parents at a very early age and kept in cages begin 'collecting' in the autumn. Such animals have never known winter conditions and will not be deprived of nourishment in the coming months. Nevertheless, they 'hoard' simply for the sake of 'hoarding.'"

Summing up the contrast between man and animals, he remarks:

"The world of animals is therefore exclusively that of the present moment in the most literal sense of the word. For they can easily be diverted from even the most fascinating objects by others of more immediate appeal at the time and never afterwards return to the former."

Truly, then, man alone has a concept of "time indefinite," the ability to meditate on the past and to look toward the future, planning for it.

It is because animals live only in the present that for them death is clearly not the tragedy it is for humans. Animals seem to react to death as a natural course of events.

Take the case witnessed in Serengeti National Park involving a lioness and her three cubs.

While the lioness was away, the cubs lay hidden in a thicket. Then two male lions from another territory appeared. Finding the hidden cubs, they killed all three. They ate one, carried the other off and left the third behind. What did the lioness do when she returned and saw her remaining dead cub? She displayed no grief, no emotion, but merely sniffed at the carcass of her remaining dead cub—and then devoured it.

It is also noteworthy that animals on which lions prey do not react with terror at seeing a lion some distance away. Once a lion has gotten its meal, herds of animals soon resume their usual routine. In fact, prey animals may come within one hundred and twenty feet of a visible lion.

## MAN REACTS TO DEATH AS SOMETHING UNNATURAL

How differently humans react to death! For the majority, the death of a wife, husband or child is the most upsetting experience of a lifetime. Man's entire emotional makeup is jarred for a long time after the death of a person whom he dearly loves.

Even those persons who claim that 'death is natural to humans' find it hard to accept the idea that their own death will mean the end of everything. Observes *The Journal of Legal Medicine:* "Psychiatrists are generally agreed that there is an unconscious denial of death, even when it seems to be imminent." A young avowed atheist, for example, stated before his execution that, from a rational point of view, his death would mean 'nothing more than the definitive termination of a life that had been brief but very intense.' But then he noted that it was difficult, indeed impossible, for him to 'admit that everything would be reduced to nothingness.'

So strong is man's desire to share in future activity that a number of people have arranged to have their bodies frozen at death. The initial cost for this may run as high as $8,500, with an additional $1,000 being paid each year to keep the body frozen. Bodies have been frozen in the hope that scientists will eventually be able to bring them back to life. Of course, at the present time scientists are nowhere even near accomplishing such a thing. Yet the very thought that this might be possible has been enough to move some persons to have their bodies preserved at great cost.

Because humans find it hard to accept death as ending everything, men everywhere have a desire to perpetuate the memory of the dead and to dispose of them ceremoniously. Notes the book *Funeral Customs the World Over:*

"There is no group, however primitive at the one extreme or civilized at the other, which left freely to itself and within its means does not dispose of the bodies of its members with ceremony. So true is this universal fact of ceremonial funeralization that it seems reasonable to conclude that it flows out of human nature. It is 'natural,' normal, reasonable. It satisfies deep universal urges. To carry it out seems 'right,' and not to carry it out, particularly for those who are closely connected by family, feeling, shared living, common experience or other ties, seems 'wrong,' an unnatural omission, a matter to be apologized for or ashamed of."

What does this work conclude from the universal custom of funerals? It continues:

"So true is this that to the various definitions of man there might be added another. He is a being that buries his dead with ceremony."

Yet, despite all of this, eventually, as generations come and go, the deceased are totally forgotten. Even those who made a notable name in history centuries ago have, as actual persons, faded from the everyday memory of the living. Their influence on others is gone. For example, such powerful rulers of ancient times as Nebuchadnezzar, Alexander the Great and Julius Caesar do not affect our daily lives now even though they affected the lives of millions of their contemporaries. The hard fact that the dead are in time forgotten was acknowledged by the discerning writer of the Bible book of Ecclesiastes: "There is no remembrance of people of former times, nor will there be of those also who will come to be later. There will prove to be no remembrance even of them among those who will come to be still later on." (Ecclesiastes 1:11) The very fact that man tries everything within his power to be remembered despite his knowing that he will eventually be forgotten shows that his desire to live, if but in memory, is inherent.

## MAN'S DEATH DOES NOT SEEM TO MAKE SENSE

In view of man's general reaction to death, his amazing potential as to memory and learning ability, and his inward realization of eternity, is it not clear that he was made to live? Only when we accept the Bible's explanation that man's present dying state was never a part of God's original purpose can we make sense out of things that would otherwise be very puzzling. Take as an example the life-spans of certain plants and animals that far surpass that of man.

A tree may live for hundreds of years; some, such as sequoias and bristlecone pines, for thou-

# DOES MAN'S SHORT LIFE-SPAN MAKE SENSE?

Despite their amazing potential for learning, humans live just **70** or **80** years

Even swans are known to live over **80** years

Though unintelligent, tortoises live more than **150** years

Some trees live thousands of years

sands of years. It is not unusual for a giant tortoise to get to be more than 150 years old. Why should this be? Why should mindless trees and unreasoning tortoises outlive intelligent man?

Then, too, is not man's death a terrible waste? While a fraction of a man's knowledge and experience may have been passed on to others, for the most part these things are lost to posterity. To illustrate, a man may be an outstanding scientist, a fine architect or an accomplished musician, painter or sculptor. He may have trained others. But at his death no one has the sum total of his talents and experience. He may even have been in the process of developing something new after having solved many problems. Those who could have benefited from the knowledge and experience he gained may now have to learn through trial and error—and then have their own work cut short by death. Since the field of knowledge is very great, why should man have to labor under the handicap of being deprived of experienced people as they fall victim to death?

Additionally, to say that man was to live just a few years on earth and then to die cannot be reconciled with belief in a loving Creator. Why not? Because this would mean that the Creator cares more about certain unintelligent plants and dumb animals than he does about humans, who can express love and appreciation. It would also mean that he has little compassion for humans, who, of all earthly forms of life, are hurt most deeply by death.

Truly, if this life were all there is, and if God had indeed purposed it this way, how could we really love him? Yes, how could we be drawn to One who made it impossible for us to come to the full realization of our potential? Would it not be an unkindness to be given tremendous potential for gaining knowledge and then to be stifled in one's use of it?

However, if humans were made to continue to live, then they need an answer to the question, Why is it that man dies? And a satisfying answer is needed to help them to understand why God has allowed death to go on claiming human victims for thousands of years. This may well remove a serious obstacle standing in the way of one's coming into a fine relationship with the Creator and finding real meaning and enjoyment in life now.

But how can we be sure about the reason for death?

CHAPTER 4

# How Did Old Age and Death Come About?

THOUGH popularly accepted as normal, old age and death still puzzle man. This is evident from the fact that for centuries legends have been handed down attempting to explain why humans grow old and die.

One version of an ancient Greek myth tells of the woman Pandora who opened a box or vase that she had been told to keep closed. This act, it is said, released "Old Age," "Sickness," "Insanity" and other "Spites" that have continued to plague mankind.

In Australia, various aboriginal tribes believe

that humans originally were to live forever. But they were to keep away from a certain hollow tree. When wild bees made this tree their home, the women very much desired their honey. Disregarding the warning of the men, one woman used her tomahawk on the tree. At that, the legend says, a large bat flew out. The bat was "Death." Released from the tree, it proceeded to claim all that it touched with its wings.

It is significant that legends of other, widely scattered peoples similarly attribute death to disobedience, often with a woman initially involved.

## WHY THE SIMILARITIES?

When reading such myths, some persons may be inclined to place the Bible's explanation of the cause for old age and death in the same category. They may even point out that in some respects the myths seem to parallel the Bible account. But *why* do these similarities exist? Is it possible that these legends have a factual basis that has simply been distorted?

The Bible itself sheds light on the answers to these questions. It points to ancient Babel in Chaldea as the place from which humans who rebelled against God by defying his command were scattered. (Genesis 11:2-9) Biblical tables of genealogy show that this took place at a time when some men were alive who, as faithful servants of God, knew the truth about life and the reason for death. (Genesis 6:7, 8; 8:20, 21; 9:28; 10:1-9; 11:10-18; 1 Chronicles 1:19) The majority, however, since they themselves were showing disregard for the truth as to God's purpose for man, could hardly be expected to preserve with accuracy the truth about how death came about. As they spread out, and with the passage of time, the facts became distorted and embellished; myths developed. There is great variety in their mythical explanations of the cause of aging and death, yet a common underlying basis is discernible.

This is no mere supposition. Available evidence clearly shows that religious myths, including those about death, spring from a common source. In his book *The Worship of the Dead*, Colonel J. Garnier observes:

"Not merely Egyptians, Chaldeans, Phœnicians, Greeks and Romans, but also the Hindus, the Buddhists of China and of Tibet, the Goths, Anglo-Saxons, Druids, Mexicans and Peruvians, the Aborigines of Australia, and even the savages of the South Sea Islands, must have all derived their religious ideas from a common source and a common centre. Everywhere we find the most startling coincidences in rites, ceremonies, cus-

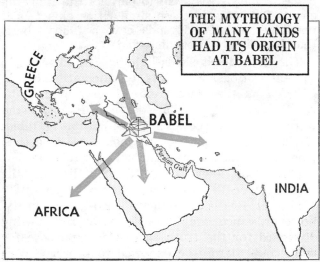

THE MYTHOLOGY OF MANY LANDS HAD ITS ORIGIN AT BABEL

toms, traditions, and in the names and relations of their respective gods and goddesses."

And what place is this common source? Does the evidence point to Chaldea, as the Bible implies? Professor George Rawlinson notes:

"The striking resemblance of the Chaldæan system to that of the Classical [primarily Greek and Roman] Mythology seems worthy of particular attention. This resemblance is too general, and too close in some respects, to allow of the supposition that mere accident has produced the coincidence. In the Pantheons of Greece and Rome, and in that of Chaldæa, the same general grouping [of gods and goddesses] is to be recognized; the same genealogical succession is not unfrequently to be traced; and in some cases even the familiar names and titles of classical divinities admit of the most curious illustration and explanation from Chaldæan sources."

What does he therefore conclude? He says:

"We can scarcely doubt but that, in some way or other, there was a communication of beliefs—a passage in very early times, from the shores of the Persian Gulf [where ancient Babel was] to the lands washed by the Mediterranean, of mythological notions and ideas."

Thus what the Bible indicates as to the development of religious concepts is found to be consistent with other historical evidence. If the Bible really does preserve with accuracy the truth that religious myths later distorted, the Bible account should appeal to our faculties of reason. The account should make sense. Does it?

### LIFE DEPENDENT ON OBEDIENCE

In discussing the reasons for aging and death, the first book of the Bible, Genesis, does not deal with some "once-upon-a-time" setting in a "dreamland," but presents a factual account. It deals with an actual place, Eden, its general geographical location being identified by certain rivers. Two of these, the Euphrates and the Tigris (Hiddekel), are known to this day. (Genesis 2:10-14; *New English Bible*) The time can be fixed by Bible chronology as the year 4026 B.C.E. or shortly thereafter. Furthermore, the Bible's reference to a first human pair is scientifically sound. Notes the publication *The Races of Mankind:*

> "The Bible story of Adam and Eve, father and mother of the whole human race, told centuries ago the same truth that science has shown today: that all the peoples of the earth are a single family and have a common origin."

After relating the manner in which the first human came to life, the Biblical account shows that the Creator, Jehovah God, started humanity off in a parklike home. He placed before man the prospect of unending life, while at the same time making its enjoyment conditional. God said to the man: "From every tree of the garden you may eat to satisfaction. But as for the tree of the knowledge of good and bad you must not eat from it, for in the day you eat from it you will positively die."—Genesis 2:16, 17.

That was a simple command. Yet is this not what we should expect? The man Adam was alone at the time. Life was simple, uncomplicated. There were no problems in making a living. There were no pressures from a greedy commercial system. Complex laws were not needed to control sinful inclinations within the first man. As a perfect man, Adam had no sinful tendencies.

Simple as this command was, it involved moral issues of serious consequence. Disobedience to God's command on the part of the first humans would have meant rebellion against Him as Ruler. How so?

It was God's prohibition that made partaking of the fruit of the "tree of the knowledge of good and bad" wrong. There were no poisonous properties in it. The fruit was wholesome, literally "good for food." (Genesis 3:6) Hence, God's prohibition regarding the tree simply emphasized man's proper dependence on his Creator as Ruler. By obedience the first man and woman could show that they respected God's right to make known to them what was "good," or divinely approved, and what was "bad," or divinely condemned. Disobedience on their part therefore would mean rebellion against God's sovereignty.

Jehovah God stated the penalty for such rebellion to be death. Was that too severe a penalty? Well, do not many nations of the world consider it within their right to designate certain crimes as capital offenses? Yet these nations cannot give nor indefinitely sustain the life of anyone. But man's Creator can. And it was because of his will that Adam and Eve came into existence. (Revelation 4:11) So was it not right for the Giver and Sustainer of life to designate disobedience to him as worthy of death? Surely! Then, too, he alone fully recognized the seriousness of the damaging effects that would result from disobedience to his law.

By obeying the prohibitive command, that first human pair, Adam and Eve, could have demonstrated their appreciation and gratitude to God for all that he had done for them. Rightly motivated obedience would have prevented them from becoming selfish and ignoring their Benefactor, God.

The Bible says
that God gave
the first humans
the prospect of
unending life

The command was of a nature that we would expect from a God of love and justice. It was not unreasonable. He did not deprive them of life's necessities. There were many other trees from which they could satisfy their need for food. Hence, neither Adam nor Eve had any reason to feel a need for the fruit of the "tree of the knowledge of good and bad."

The account shows that one day, however, while not in the company of her husband, Eve fell victim to a deception and partook of the forbidden fruit.* Later she succeeded in persuading her husband to join her in breaking God's law. —Genesis 3:1-6.

Now, it might be argued that God could have taken a permissive attitude toward this rebellion of the first humans. It might be suggested that he could have shut his eyes to their wrongdoing, leaving it unpunished. But would that have been the best course? Is it not true that failure to uphold law among humans today has led to disrespect for just laws and to increasing crime and violence? For God to have left the wrongdoing of Adam and Eve unpunished would have meant emboldening them and their descendants to carry on further lawlessness. This would have made God share responsibility for such acts.

Then, too, permissiveness would have called into question the reliability of God's word. It would have made it appear that he does not mean what he says and that his laws can therefore be violated with impunity.

Thus it becomes clear that it was the only right and just thing for God to uphold his law

---

* The details about this deception and its instigator are discussed in chapter 10.

and to let the first humans suffer the rightful consequences of their willful, deliberate disobedience. Not to be overlooked is that there is no evidence of any repentance on their part. They gave no evidence of a change of heart.

## THE BASIC REASON—SIN

By their rebellion against God, Adam and Eve cut themselves off from a good relationship with him. They did not possess an indestructible, immortal life. The Bible says that by means of his power God 'keeps the sun, moon and stars standing forever, to time indefinite.' (Psalm 148:3-6) So, too, with the first human pair. They were dependent upon God for continued life.

By refusing to submit to God's law, Adam and Eve deprived themselves of his sustaining power. Moreover, alienated from God, they were without his divine direction and guidance. In time, then, the sin that had alienated Adam and Eve from God brought about their death.

However, following their transgression against God they still had in themselves tremendous potential for life. This is evident from the historical record, which shows that Adam lived for 930 years. (Genesis 5:5) Yet, fulfilled upon Adam was the warning: "In the day you eat from [the tree of the knowledge of good and bad] you will positively die," for God sentenced Adam to death on that day.—Genesis 2:17.

Through his disobedience, Adam, as the progenitor of the human family, brought death, not only to himself, but also to his unborn offspring. That is why the Bible says: "Through one man sin entered into the world and death through sin, and thus death spread to all men because they had all sinned."—Romans 5:12.

Having forfeited perfection, Adam could not pass it on to his offspring. From the start his children were born with weaknesses. The out-workings of sin in his body made it impossible for him to father offspring without limitations and weaknesses. This harmonizes with the Bible's statement at Job 14:4: "Who can produce some-one clean out of someone unclean? There is not one." Hence, the aging and death of humans today can be traced initially to the sin inherited from Adam. As his offspring, they are receiving the wages that sin pays—death.—Romans 6:23.

What does that really mean? Does death mark the end of all one's life processes, or is there some part of man that lives on? Does conscious exis-tence continue after the death of the body?

## CHAPTER 5

# What Is This Thing Called "Soul"?

WHAT are you? Are you, in effect, two persons in one—a human body with a brain, heart, eyes, ears, tongue, and so forth, but also having within you an invisible spiritual person completely separate from your fleshly organism and that is called the "soul"? If so, what happens when you die? Does just your body die, while the soul continues living? How can you know for sure?

Nearly all religions teach that, in the case of humans, death is not the end of all existence.

This is the case, not just in so-called Christian lands of North and South America, Europe and Australia, but also in non-Christian countries of Asia and Africa. Notes the book *Funeral Customs the World Over:* "People of most cultures believe that at death something which leaves the body has ongoing life."

Belief in the immortality of the soul is very prominent among non-Christian religions. For example, the most esteemed of sacred Hindu writings, *The Bhagavad Gita,* specifically refers to the soul as deathless. It presents this as justification for killing in war, saying:

"These bodies come to an end,
    It is declared, of the eternal embodied (soul),
Which is indestructible and unfathomable.
    Therefore fight, son of Bharata!

Who believes him a slayer,
    And who thinks him slain,
Both these understand not:
    He slays not, is not slain.

He is not born, nor does he ever die;
    Nor, having come to be, will he ever more come
        not to be.
Unborn, eternal, everlasting, this ancient one
    Is not slain when the body is slain."
—*The Bhagavad Gita,* II, 18-20.

But what is the soul here spoken of? Though strong believers in the immortality of the human soul, Hindus describe its nature in vague terms. Says the publication *Hinduism,* by Swami Vivekananda:

"The Hindu believes that every soul is a circle whose circumference is nowhere, though its centre is located in the body; and that death only means the change of this centre from one body to another. Nor is the soul bound by the conditions of matter. In its very essence, it is free, unbounded, holy, pure, and perfect. But somehow or other it finds itself bound down by matter, and thinks of itself as matter."

What, then, is the general belief among members of Christendom's churches? Professor Cullmann (Theological faculty of the University of Basel and of the Sorbonne in Paris) states:

"If we were to ask an ordinary Christian today (whether well-read Protestant or Catholic, or not) what he conceived to be the New Testament teaching concerning the fate of man after death, with few exceptions we should get the answer: 'The immortality of the soul.'"

When asked about the nature of the "soul," members of Christendom's churches, too, answer in vague, obscure terms. They have no clearer concept of an immortal soul than do adherents of non-Christian religions. This gives rise to the question, Does the Bible teach that the soul is an immortal part of man?

## IS THE SOUL IMMORTAL?

In the Bible the word "soul" appears in many translations as a rendering for the Hebrew word ne'phesh and the Greek word psy·khe'. (See, for example, Ezekiel 18:4 and Matthew 10:28 in the Authorized Version, New English Bible, Revised Standard Version and Douay Version.) These same Hebrew and Greek terms have also been translated as "being," "creature" and "person." Regardless of whether your Bible consistently renders the original-language words as "soul" (as does the New World Translation), an examination of texts where the words ne'phesh and psy·khe' appear will help you to see what these terms meant to God's people of ancient times. Thus you can determine for yourself the true nature of the soul.

Describing the creation of the first man, Adam, the opening book of the Bible says: "Jehovah God proceeded to form the man out of dust from the ground and to blow into his nostrils the breath of life, and the man came to be a living soul [ne'phesh]." (Genesis 2:7) We may note that the Bible does not say that 'man received a soul,' but that "man *came to be* a living soul."

Did first-century Christian teaching differ from this concept of "soul"? No. In what is commonly called the "New Testament," the statement about Adam's creation is quoted as fact: "It is even so written: 'The first man Adam became a living soul.'" (1 Corinthians 15:45) In the original language of this text the word for "soul," *psy·khe'*, appears. Accordingly, in this scripture the Greek word *psy·khe'*, like the Hebrew word *ne'phesh*, designates, not some invisible spirit residing in man, but man himself. Rightly, then, certain Bible translators have chosen to use such words as "being," "creature" and "person" in their renderings of Genesis 2:7 and 1 Corinthians 15:45. —*New English Bible, Young's Literal Translation, Revised Standard Version;* compare *The Bible in Living English,* which uses "person" at Genesis 2:7 but "soul" at 1 Corinthians 15:45.

It is also noteworthy that the terms *ne'phesh* and *psy·khe'* are applied to animals. Concerning the creation of sea and land creatures, the Bible says: "God went on to say: 'Let the waters swarm forth a swarm of living souls ["creatures," *New English Bible*] and let flying creatures fly over the earth' . . . God proceeded to create the great sea monsters and every living soul that moves about . . . 'Let the earth put forth living souls according to their kinds, domestic animal and moving animal and wild beast of the earth according to its kind.' "—Genesis 1:20-24.

Such references to animals as being souls are not limited to the opening book of the Bible. From the first book of the Holy Scriptures to the very last book, animals continue to be designated as souls. It is written: "Take away from the men of war who went out on the expedition one soul [ne'phesh] out of five hundred, of humankind and of the herd and of the asses and of the flock." (Numbers 31:28) "The righteous one is caring for the soul [ne'phesh] of his domestic animal." (Proverbs 12:10) "Every living soul [psy·khe'] died, yes, the things in the sea."—Revelation 16:3.

The application of the word "soul" to animals is very appropriate. It is in agreement with what is thought to be the basic meaning of the Hebrew term ne'phesh. This word is understood to be derived from a root meaning "to breathe." Hence, in a literal sense, a soul is a "breather," and animals are indeed breathers. They are living, breathing creatures.

As to their application to humans, the words ne'phesh and psy·khe' are repeatedly used in such a way as to mean the entire person. We read in the Bible that the human soul is born. (Genesis 46:18) It can eat or fast. (Leviticus 7:20; Psalm 35:13) It can weep and faint. (Jeremiah 13:17; Jonah 2:7) A soul can swear, crave things and give way to fear. (Leviticus 5:4; Deuteronomy 12:20; Acts 2:43) A person might kidnap a soul. (Deuteronomy 24:7) The soul can be pursued and put in irons. (Psalm 7:5; 105:18) Are these not the kind of things done by or to *fleshly* people?

THEY ARE
ALL
SOULS

Do not such passages of Scripture clearly establish that the human soul is the entire man?

Numerous twentieth-century Bible scholars, Catholic, Protestant and Jewish, have been brought to this conclusion. Note their comments:

"The famous verse in Genesis [2:7] does not say, as is often supposed, that man consists of body and soul; it says that Yahweh shaped man, earth from the ground, and then proceeded to animate the inert figure with living breath blown into his nostrils, so that man became a living *being*, which is all that *nephesh* [soul] here means."—H. Wheeler Robinson of Regent's Park College, London, in *Zeitschrift für die alttestamentliche Wissenschaft* (Journal for the Old Testament Science), Vol. 41 (1923).

"Man must not be thought of as *having* a soul: he *is* a soul."—E. F. Kevan, Principal of the London Bible College, in *The New Bible Commentary* (1965), 2d ed., p. 78.

"The soul in the O[ld] T[estament] means not a part of man, but the whole man—man as a living being. Similarly, in the N[ew] T[estament] it signifies human life: the life of an individual, conscious subject."—*New Catholic Encyclopedia* (1967), Vol. 13, p. 467.

"The Bible does not say we have a soul. 'Nefesh' is the person himself, his need for food, the very blood in his veins, his being."—Dr. H. M. Orlinsky of Hebrew Union College, quoted in New York *Times*, October 12, 1962.

Does it seem strange to you that scholars of various religious persuasions are now saying that the soul is man himself? Is this what you have been taught? Or, have you been taught that the soul is an immortal part of man? If so, what effect has this teaching had on you? Has it moved you to spend money for religious purposes that you would otherwise have used for necessities of life? Could it be that your church has

been dishonest in its teaching? Who is right
—the church or its scholars?

If the scholars are right in saying that the
human soul is the entire person, including his
fleshly body, we should expect the Bible to refer
to the soul as being mortal. Does it? Yes. The
Bible speaks of 'holding back,' 'rescuing' and
'saving' a *ne'phesh* or soul from death. (Psalm
78:50; 116:8; James 5:20) We also read: "Let
us not strike his soul fatally." (Genesis 37:21)
"The manslayer must flee there who fatally strikes
a soul unintentionally." (Numbers 35:11) "Their
soul will die in youth." (Job 36:14) "The soul
that is sinning—it itself will die."—Ezekiel 18:4,
20.

But is it possible that at least in a few Scriptural references the original-language words rendered "soul" designate something that leaves the
body at death and is immortal? What about such
texts as the following? "As her soul was going
out (because she died) she called his name Ben-
oni." (Genesis 35:18) "My God, please, cause the
soul of this child to come back within him."
(1 Kings 17:21) "Stop raising a clamor, for his
soul is in him." (Acts 20:10) Do not these passages indicate that the soul is something that
exists independently of the body?

The text at Job 33:22, written in poetic style,
provides a key to understanding these passages.
There "soul" and "life" are placed in parallel, so
that the two words could be interchanged without
changing the sense of the passage. We read:
"His *soul* draws near to the pit, and his *life* to
those inflicting death." From this parallel we can
see that the word "soul" can mean life as a person
and, therefore, the departure of the soul can be

understood to refer to the end of life as a person.

To illustrate: A man might say that his dog 'lost its life' when it was hit by a truck. Does he mean that this animal's life left the body and continued existing? No, he is simply using a figure of speech indicating that the animal died. The same is true when we speak of a man as 'losing his life.' We do not mean that his life exists independently of the body. Similarly, 'to lose one's soul' means to 'lose one's life as a soul' and carries no meaning of continued existence after death. Recognizing this, *The Interpreter's Dictionary of the Bible* states:

> "The 'departure' of the *nephesh* [soul] must be viewed as a figure of speech, for it does not continue to exist independently of the body, but dies with it (Num. 31:19; Judg. 16:30; Ezek. 13:19). No biblical text authorizes the statement that the 'soul' is separated from the body at the moment of death."

## THE SOURCE OF THE BELIEF

The Scriptural evidence is unmistakably clear that man does not have an immortal soul but is himself a soul. How, then, did this belief about an immortal soul find its way into the teachings of Christendom's churches? Today it is frankly acknowledged that this has come about through the influence of pagan Grecian philosophy. Writes Professor Douglas T. Holden in his book *Death Shall Have No Dominion:*

> "Christian theology has become so fused with Greek philosophy that it has reared individuals who are a mixture of nine parts Greek thought to one part Christian thought."

The Catholic magazine *Commonweal,* in its issue of January 15, 1971, confessed that the idea of an immortal soul was a concept that "the late

Jews and early Christians inherited from Athens."

Who is to blame for this mixture of pagan Greek and Christian thought? Is it not the religious clergy? Surely the church members did not on their own come up with this teaching, one that Bible scholars now openly admit to be unscriptural.

But from where did the ancient Greeks get their basic religious foundation? As has already been pointed out, there is strong evidence that the religious concepts of the Greeks and other peoples were influenced by the Babylonians. And as to Babylonian beliefs about the soul note what *The International Standard Bible Encyclopædia* says:

> "After death the souls of men were supposed to continue in existence. . . . The Babylonians . . . placed often with the dead articles which might be used in his future existence. . . . In the future world there seem to have been distinctions made among the dead. Those who fell in battle seem to have had special favor. They received fresh water to drink, while those who had no posterity to put offerings at their graves suffered sore and many deprivations."

So the Greeks could easily have gotten their basic ideas about the immortality of the soul from Babylon, which ideas were then enlarged upon by the Greek philosophers.

Something similar appears to have taken place in connection with the non-Christian religions still in existence today. For example, a comparison of the ancient civilization of the Indus Valley, where Hinduism is the dominant religion, with that of Mesopotamia reveals notable similarities. These include structures like the religious ziggurat platforms of Mesopotamia and pictographic signs bearing a strong resemblance to early Mesopotamian forms. On the basis of his study, the noted Assyriologist Samuel N. Kramer suggested that the Indus Valley was settled by a people who fled from Mesopotamia when the Sumerians took control of the area. It is not difficult to understand, then, where Hinduism got its belief in an undying soul.

The evidence thus points to Babylon as the most ancient source from which belief in the immortality of the human soul radiated to the ends of the earth. And there at Babylon, according to the Bible, a rebellion against God occurred. In itself that would be reason enough to view the doctrine of an immortal soul with reservations. But do not forget that, as we have already seen, this teaching is also in direct conflict with the Bible.

Furthermore, is not the idea that the soul is immortal contrary to what you personally have observed? For example, what happens when a person is knocked unconscious, faints, or is placed under an anesthetic at a hospital? If his "soul" is really something separate from the body and is able to function intelligently apart from the body, so that even death itself does not affect its existence and its functions, why is it that during such period of unconsciousness the person is completely unaware of all activity around him? Why is it that he must be told afterward what happened during that time? If his "soul" can see, hear, feel and think after death, as religions generally teach, why does something far less drastic than death, such as a period of unconsciousness, stop all these functions?

Also, a dead body, whether it be that of a human or of an animal, eventually returns to the elements of the ground. Nothing about death even hints at there being an immortal soul that lives on.

### EFFECT OF THE DOCTRINE ABOUT
### THE SOUL'S IMMORTALITY

What a person believes about the soul is of no little consequence.

The teaching of the immortality of the human soul has been used to override the conscience of people in times of war. Religious leaders have made it appear that taking life is not so bad, as those slain do not really die after all. And those who die in battle against the enemy are promised bliss. Typical are remarks such as those reported on in the New York *Times* of September 11, 1950: "Sorrowing parents whose sons have been drafted or recalled for combat duty were told yesterday in St. Patrick's Cathedral that death in battle was part of God's plan for populating 'the kingdom of Heaven.'" The idea here expressed differs little from the ancient Babylonian teaching that the war dead gained special favors.

Misrepresentations of what the Bible says about the soul have thus contributed toward the placing of a cheapened value on human life and have made people feel dependent on the great religious systems that have falsely claimed to care for their souls.

Knowing these things, what will you do? It is obvious that the true God, who is himself "the God of truth" and who hates lies, will not look with favor on persons who cling to organizations that teach falsehood. (Psalm 31:5; Proverbs 6: 16-19; Revelation 21:8) And, really, would you want to be even associated with a religion that had not been honest with you?

## CHAPTER 6

# *The Spirit That Returns to God*

THERE should be no question in the mind of any sincere investigator that what the Bible speaks of as "soul" is not some immortal part of man that continues conscious existence after death. Yet when shown the overwhelming evidence about the true nature of the soul, some persons present other arguments in an effort to support their belief that *something* within man has continued existence after death.

One Biblical text that is often used is Ecclesiastes 12:7, which reads: "The dust returns to the earth just as it happened to be and the spirit itself returns to the true God who gave it." In his *Commentary,* Wesleyan Methodist theologian Adam Clarke writes concerning this verse: "Here the wise man makes a most evident distinction between the body and the soul: they are not the same; they are not both matter. The body, which is matter, returns to dust, its original; but the spirit, which is *immaterial,* returns to God." Similarly, *A Catholic Commentary on Holy Scripture* says: "The soul goes back to God." Thus both commentaries imply that the soul and the spirit are the same.

Interestingly, though, other Roman Catholic and Protestant scholars present an entirely different view. In the "Glossary of Biblical Theology Terms" appearing in the Catholic *New American Bible* (published by P. J. Kenedy & Sons, New

York, 1970), we read: "When 'spirit' is used in contrast with 'flesh,' . . . the aim is not to distinguish a material from an immaterial part of man . . . 'Spirit' does not mean soul." At Ecclesiastes 12:7 this translation uses, not the word "spirit," but the expression "life breath." The Protestant *Interpreter's Bible* observes regarding the writer of Ecclesiastes: "Koheleth does not mean that man's personality continues to exist." In view of such different conclusions, can we be sure just what the spirit is and in what sense it returns to God?

At Ecclesiastes 12:1-7 the effects of old age and death are portrayed in poetic language. After death, the body eventually decomposes and again becomes a part of the dust of the earth. The "spirit," on the other hand, "returns to the true God." So man's death is linked with the spirit's returning to God, this indicating that man's life in some way depends upon that spirit.

In the original-language text of Ecclesiastes 12:7, the Hebrew word translated "spirit" or "life breath" is *ru'ahh*. The corresponding Greek term is *pneu'ma*. While our life does depend on the breathing process, the English word "breath" (as numerous translators often render the words *ru'ahh* and *pneu'ma*) is not always a suitable alternate translation for "spirit." Furthermore, other Hebrew and Greek words, namely, *ne·sha·mah'* (Hebrew) and *pno·e'* (Greek), are also translated as "breath." (See Genesis 2:7 and Acts 17:25.) It is nevertheless noteworthy that, in using "breath" as an alternate rendering for "spirit," translators are showing that the original-language terms apply to something that has no personality but is essential for the continuance of life.

## THE SPIRIT IDENTIFIED

That man's life depends on the spirit (*ru'ahh* or *pneu'ma*) is definitely stated in the Bible. We read: "If you [Jehovah] take away their spirit [*ru'ahh*], they expire, and back to their dust they go." (Psalm 104:29) "The body without spirit [*pneu'ma*] is dead." (James 2:26) Hence, the spirit is that which animates the body.

But this animating force is not simply breath. Why not? Because life remains in the body cells for a brief period after breathing stops. For this reason efforts at resuscitation can succeed, also body organs can be transplanted from one person to another. But these things have to be done quickly. Once the life-force is gone from the cells of the body, efforts to prolong life are futile. All the breath in the world could not revive even as much as one cell. Viewed in this light, the "spirit" evidently is an invisible life-force, active in every living cell of man's body.

Is this life-force active only in man? What is stated in the Bible can help us to reach a sound conclusion on this. Regarding the destruction of human and animal life in a global flood, the Bible reports: "Everything in which the breath [*ne·sha·mah'*] of the force [*ru'ahh*, spirit] of life was active in its nostrils, namely, all that were on the dry ground, died." (Genesis 7:22) At Ecclesiastes 3:19 the same basic point is made in connection with death: "There is an eventuality as respects the sons of mankind and an eventuality as respects the beast, and they have the same eventuality. As the one dies, so the other dies;

and they all have but one spirit [*ru'ahh*], so
that there is no superiority of the man over the
beast." Accordingly, man is not superior to animals when it comes to the spirit animating his
body. The same invisible spirit or life-force is
common to both.

In a sense, the spirit or life-force active in both
animals and man might be compared to a flow
of electrons or electricity through a machine or
an appliance. The invisible electricity may be used
to perform various functions, depending upon the
type of machine or appliance being energized.
Stoves can be made to produce heat, fans to
produce wind, computers to solve problems, and
television sets to reproduce figures, voices and
other sounds. The same invisible force that produces sound in one appliance can produce heat
in another, mathematical computations in another. But does the electric current ever take on
the often complex characteristics of the machines
or appliances in which it functions or is active?
No, it remains simply electricity—a mere force
or form of energy.

Similarly, both humans and animals "have but
one spirit," one activating force. The spirit or
life-force that enables man to carry out functions
of life in no way differs from the spirit that makes
it possible for animals to do so. That spirit does
not retain the characteristics of the dead body's
cells. For example, in the case of brain cells, the
spirit does not retain the information stored there
and continue thought processes apart from these
cells. The Bible tells us: "His spirit [*ru'ahh*] goes
out, he goes back to his ground; in that day his
thoughts do perish."—Psalm 146:4.

This being the case, the return of the *ru'ahh*

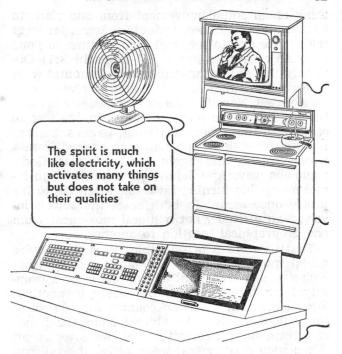

The spirit is much like electricity, which activates many things but does not take on their qualities

or spirit to God simply could not mean the continuance of conscious existence. The spirit does not continue human thought processes. It is only a life-force that has no conscious existence apart from a body.

### HOW THE SPIRIT RETURNS TO GOD

How, then, does this invisible, impersonal force or spirit return to God? Does it return to his literal presence in heaven?

The way in which the Bible uses the word "return" does not require that we, in each case, think of an actual movement from one place to another. For instance, unfaithful Israelites were told: " 'Return to me, and I will return to you,' Jehovah of armies has said." (Malachi 3:7) Obviously this did not mean that the Israelites were to leave the earth and come into the very presence of God. Nor did it mean that God would leave his position in the heavens and begin dwelling on earth with the Israelites. Rather, Israel's "returning" to Jehovah meant a turning around from a wrong course and again conforming to God's righteous way. And Jehovah's "returning" to Israel meant his turning favorable attention to his people once again. In both cases the return involved an attitude, not a literal movement from one geographical location to another.

That the return of something does not require actual movement might be illustrated by what happens in a transferal of a business or a property from the control of one party to another. For example, in a certain country the control of the railroads might be shifted from the hands of private enterprise to those of the government. When such a transferal takes place, the railroad equipment and even all the records may remain where they are. It is the *authority* over them that changes hands.

So it is in the case of the spirit or life-force. At death no actual movement from the earth to the heavenly realm need occur for it to 'return to God.' But the gift or grant of existence as an intelligent creature, as enjoyed once by the dead person, now reverts to God. That which is needed to animate the person, namely, the spirit or life-force, is in God's hands.—Psalm 31:5; Luke 23:46.

The situation might be compared to that of an

accused man who says to a judge, 'My life is in your hands.' He means that what will become of his life rests with the judge. The accused has no choice in the matter. It is out of his hands.

Similarly, in the case of a dead man, he does not have control over his spirit or life-force. It has returned to God in the sense that he controls the future life prospects of the individual. It is up to God to decide as to whether he will restore the spirit or life-force to the deceased.

But does this necessarily shut out all possibility of life after death? Is there not something else to consider?

### WHAT ABOUT REBIRTH OR REINCARNATION?

Millions of persons of various religious persuasions, whether called Christian or non-Christian, believe that humans had an existence prior to their present life and will continue to live after they die. Though their concepts vary greatly, they share in common the conviction that some part of man is reborn or reincarnated in another body.

Presenting one line of argument in favor of the belief in rebirth, *A Manual of Buddhism* states: "Sometimes we get strange experiences which cannot be explained but by rebirth. How often do we meet persons whom we have never before met and yet inwardly feel that they are quite familiar to us? How often do we visit places and yet feel impressed that we are perfectly acquainted with their surroundings?"

Have you ever experienced such things? After meeting a person, have you ever had the feeling that you have known him for a long time? What accounts for such an experience?

There are many similarities in people. Perhaps, after some thought, you yourself realized that the person had personality traits and physical features resembling those of a relative or a friend.

Likewise you may have lived in a particular city or seen pictures of it. Then, when visiting another city, you may note certain similarities so that you feel that you are not really amid strange and unfamiliar surroundings.

So, then, is it not reasonable to conclude that feelings of familiarity about previously unknown people and places are, not the product of some past life, but a result of experiences in the present life? Really, if all people had actually had previous existences, should they not all be aware of this? Why, then, do millions not even have the slightest sense or thought of having lived an earlier life? Furthermore, how can a person avoid the mistakes of his earlier lives if he cannot even recall them? Of what benefit would such previous lives be?

Some may offer the explanation that 'life would be a burden if people knew the details of their previous existences.' That is the way Mohandas K. Gandhi expressed it, saying: "It is nature's kindness that we do not remember past births. Where is the good either of knowing in detail the numberless births we have gone through? Life would be a burden if we carried such a tremendous load of memories. A wise man deliberately forgets many things, even as a lawyer forgets the cases and their details as soon as they are disposed of." That is an interesting explanation, but does it rest on a solid foundation?

While our ability to recall many things that we have experienced may be limited, our minds are certainly not *totally blank* respecting them. A lawyer may forget the precise details of certain cases, but the experience gained in handling them becomes part of his fund of knowledge. He would indeed be at a great disadvantage if he actually forgot everything. Then, too, which causes people greater disturbance—a poor memory or a good memory? Is not an old man who has a good recall of his fund of knowledge and experience far better off than an old man who has practically forgotten everything?

Really, what "kindness" would there be in having to learn all over again things that one had already learned during a previous existence? Would you consider it "nature's kindness" if every ten years of your life you forgot practically everything you knew and had to start learning a language again and then begin building up a fund of knowledge and experience, only to have it eradicated? Would this not be frustrating? Would this not result in terrible setbacks? Why, then, imagine that it happens every seventy or eighty years? Can you feature that a loving God could have made such rebirth part of his purpose for mankind?

Many who accept the doctrine of rebirth believe that those leading a bad life will be reborn in a lower caste or as insects, birds or beasts. Yet why is it, then, that there is a big *human* population explosion at a time when crime and violence are increasing on an unprecedented scale? Also, why can even those in the lowest caste excel when given educational opportunities? For example, the New York *Times* of October 26, 1973, reported that a sixteen-year-old girl of low caste was the brightest girl in the school at Kallipashim,

India. She was smarter than a girl of the highest caste, a Brahman. How might this be explained? Is it not true that the doctrine of rebirth or reincarnation cannot provide satisfying explanations for such things?

Think, too, of the fruitage that such teaching has produced. Has it not deprived many humans of a dignified standing, forcing them to take menial jobs under poor working conditions, with little possibility of improving their lot in life through education?

### DOES THE BIBLE TEACH REBIRTH?

Of course, some persons might point out that logical deductions do not necessarily rule out the possibility of rebirth. Their reply to the aforementioned arguments might be: 'Even the Bible teaches rebirth. This is just one of many things that humans cannot fully explain.'

Since believers in rebirth do bring the Bible into the discussion, we should want to consider what it does say. Just what Biblical evidence is there for the belief in rebirth? The book *What Is Buddhism?* answers: "For the Christian reader we would point out that [the doctrine of rebirth] is clearly present in such mutilated fragments of Christ's teachings as are still extant. Consider, for example, the widely current rumours that he was John the Baptist, Jeremiah or Elijah come again (Matt. xvi, 13-16). Even Herod seemed to think that he was 'John the Baptist risen from the dead.'"

What about such arguments? Did Jesus Christ himself claim to be John the Baptist, Jeremiah or Elijah? No, these claims were made by persons who did not accept Jesus for what he really was, namely, the promised Messiah or Christ. Jesus simply could not have been John the Baptist, for when about thirty years of age the younger man, Jesus, was baptized by John, who was older. (Matthew 3:13-17; Luke 3:21-23) King Herod came up with the unreasoning conclusion that Jesus was John raised from the dead, because of his feelings of extreme guilt for having executed John.

But are there not direct statements of Jesus Christ that are viewed as supporting belief in rebirth or reincarnation? Yes, there is one. On one occasion Jesus Christ linked John the Baptist with the ancient Hebrew prophet Elijah, saying: "Elijah has already come and they did not recognize him but did with him the things they wanted. . . . Then the disciples perceived that he spoke to them about John the Baptist." (Matthew 17:12, 13) In stating, "Elijah has already come," did Jesus mean that John the Baptist was Elijah reborn?

The answer to this question must be determined on the basis of what the Bible says as a whole. Many Jews back in the time of Jesus' earthly ministry did think that Elijah would come back literally. And the prophecy of Malachi pointed forward to the time when Jehovah God would send the prophet Elijah. (Malachi 4:5) John the Baptist, however, did not view himself as Elijah in person or as a reincarnation of that Hebrew prophet. On one occasion certain Jews asked him, "Are you Elijah?" John replied, "I am not." (John 1:21) It had, however, been foretold that John would prepare the way before the Messiah "with Elijah's spirit and power." (Luke 1:17) Accordingly, when Jesus linked John the Baptist with Elijah he was merely showing how the prophecy was fulfilled in John who did a *work like that* of Elijah of old.

Another passage of Scripture appealed to by believers in reincarnation is Romans 9:11-13: "When [Esau and Jacob] had not yet been born nor had practiced anything good or vile, in order that the purpose of God respecting the choosing might continue dependent, not upon works, but upon the One who calls, it was said to [Rebekah]: 'The older will be the slave of the younger.' Just as it is written [at Malachi 1:2, 3]: 'I loved Jacob, but Esau I hated.' " Does this passage not show that God's choosing was based on what Jacob and Esau had done during lives prior to their being born to Rebekah?

Why not reread it? Note that it specifically says that God's choosing was made *before* either one had practiced good or bad. So God's choice did not depend upon a record of past works in some earlier life.

On what basis, then, could God make a choice before the birth of the boys? The Bible reveals that God is able to see the embryo and, therefore, knows the genetic makeup of humans before birth. (Psalm 139:16) Exercising his foreknowledge, God perceived how the two boys would be basically as to temperament and personality and thus he could make a choice of the one who might be more suitable for the superior blessing. The record made by the two boys in life confirms the wisdom of God's choice. While Jacob demonstrated spiritual interests and faith in God's promises, Esau manifested a materialistic bent and lack of appreciation for sacred things.—Hebrews 11:21; 12:16, 17.

As to the apostle Paul's quotation from Malachi about God's 'loving Jacob' and 'hating Esau,' this, too, relates to Jehovah's view of them based on their genetic makeup. While recorded by Malachi many centuries after their lifetime, the statement confirmed what God had indicated about the boys before their birth.

A question raised by Jesus' disciples is yet another example cited by some in support of reincarnation. Regarding a man blind from birth, the disciples asked: "Who sinned, this man or his parents, so that he was born blind?" (John 9:2) Do these words not reveal that the man must have had a previous existence?

No! Jesus Christ did not go along with any suggestion that the child developing in the womb of its mother had sinned of itself before birth. Jesus said: "Neither this man sinned nor his parents, but it was in order that the works of God might be made manifest in his case." (John 9:3) That is to say, human imperfections and defects such as this man's blindness provided the opportunity for the works of God to become manifest in the form of a miraculous cure. Had no one ever been born blind, humans would not have come to know that God can give sight to one born blind. Jehovah God, in allowing a sinful human race to come into existence, has used their imperfections and defects to show what he can do for them.

So while there may be Bible texts that some persons think support the concept of rebirth, closer examination indicates otherwise. In fact, nowhere in the Bible do we find any mention of the rebirth or transmigration of a soul, spirit or something else that survives the death of the body. Some have tried to 'read into' the Holy Scriptures the idea of rebirth or reincarnation. It is not a Bible doctrine.

The Bible clearly shows that conscious existence does not continue by means of a soul or spirit that leaves the body at death. When sentencing the first man to death for disobedience, God did not set before him any prospect of rebirth or reincarnation. Adam was told: "In the sweat of your face you will eat bread until you return to the ground, for out of it you were taken. For dust you are and to dust you will return." (Genesis 3:19) Yes, the man was to return to the lifeless dust of the ground.

Are we, then, to understand that this life is all there is? Or, is there a provision for future life that is available in some other way? Might this provision make it necessary for the living to help the dead, or are the dead beyond any help from the living?

**CHAPTER 7**

# Do the Dead Need Your Help?

"TO SERVE those now dead as if they were living," says an old Chinese proverb, "is the highest achievement of true filial piety." If the dead truly exist in another realm and can benefit from the services of those remaining on earth, it would be a loving thing to show concern for them.

Of course, many people simply go through the motions of observing ancient traditions, though not really being firm believers in continued existence after death. But others are convinced that the dead need their help.

Millions of persons throughout most of Asia and parts of Africa believe that they must pay homage to dead ancestors all their life. Before the ancestral tablets of their deceased relatives, they burn incense, pray, place flowers and even offer food. It is thought that such veneration will help the dead to enjoy a pleasant existence in the next life and prevent them from becoming hostile spirits.

Especially in connection with mourning and the funeral do the survivors put forth costly efforts to help the deceased. Consider the following traditional practices that were carried out in the Orient upon the death of a prominent governmental adviser:

Buddhist priests handled the rites. Firecrackers were set off to chase away evil spirits. Rice paper containing prayers was burned, in the belief that this would benefit the spirit of the dead man. Food, drink and tobacco were placed near the corpse so that the spirit could refresh itself whenever it chose to do so.

Thereafter the body was placed in a casket, which remained in a room of the funeral home for forty-nine days. For six days the eldest son mourned there. On the seventh day he returned home to sleep, bathe and change clothes. The cycle of six days of mourning and one day of rest was then repeated for the full course of the forty-nine days. Practically without any break in the entire period, firecrackers were set off, while flutes, drums and crashing cymbals resounded around the clock.

The forty-ninth day witnessed the impressive funeral march. Bands played. Along the route firecrackers strung on telephone poles, lampposts and trees were set off. Food, drink and tobacco were put on the altar tables, and paper containing prayers, as well as joss sticks, was burned in the little shrines set up all along the route. Attractive floats of paper, gold leaf and bamboo added to the colorfulness of the funeral march. Many of the mourners carried lanterns, the purpose of such lanterns being to light the way for the spirit of the dead man. At the graveside the beautiful floats, representing palaces, airplanes, ships, armies, servants and other things, were burned.

In the case of persons having lesser means and prominence, similar procedures are followed but on a much smaller scale. For example, fewer and less elaborate paper items are burned.

Belief in a purgatory is the underlying basis for such burning of paper items. After a person's death, the spirit is believed to wander in purgatory for two years, but needing help to enter heaven. The offerings made in the form of paper items are designed to show that the dead man lived a good life and has everything needed to function in the next world. This being the case, many Chinese believe, his spirit should be freed from purgatory sooner.

How do you react to such elaborate and costly ceremonies? Would you share in similar practices? If so, why?

If you believe that the dead need your help, what positive evidence do you have that something conscious survives the death of the body? What makes you sure that the means used to help the dead are effective? How, for example, could one prove that lanterns light the way for a spirit, that firecrackers chase away evil spirits and that burned paper items can help the spirit of the deceased to enter celestial bliss? What basis is there for claiming that such things are effective means for helping the spirits of the dead?

While religious ceremonies to help the dead may be quite different in your area, could anyone prove to your satisfaction that what is done brings beneficial results?

It is worth while, too, to consider how much justice and fairness are found in these efforts to help the dead. Those having great wealth naturally can buy far more firecrackers, paper items or other things supposed to aid the dead. What, then, of the poor person? Though he might have lived a good life, he would be at a disadvantage if no one did anything after his death. Also, the poor person who buys things to aid the dead labors under a great financial burden, while the rich person is only slightly affected.

How do you feel about such obvious partiality? Would you be drawn to a god that would favor the rich over the poor without consideration for what they are as persons? The God of the Bible shows no such partiality. Of him, the Holy Scriptures say: "There is no partiality with God." —Romans 2:11.

Now suppose a person realized that religious ceremonies in behalf of the dead were valueless, completely out of harmony with the will of the impartial God. Would it be reasonable for him to engage in them just for the sake of tradition and to avoid being different from his neighbors?

Is it logical to support religious ceremonies that one considers to be a falsehood? Is it right to go along with something that favors the rich and puts a hardship on the poor?

## CHRISTENDOM'S BELIEF IN PURGATORY

The belief that the dead need help to get out of purgatory is not limited to non-Christian religions. The *New Catholic Encyclopedia* states:

"The souls in purgatory can be helped by works of piety, such as prayer, indulgences, alms, fasting, and sacrifices. . . . While one cannot dictate that God apply the satisfactory value of his works to the poor souls, he may certainly hope that God will hear his petitions and help the members of the Church suffering."

How strong a guarantee is offered that such

Taoist rites, said to release a soul from purgatory

Catholic rites, said to aid souls in purgatory

efforts will bring benefit? The *Encyclopedia* continues:

"Because the application of these good works depends on one's petition to God, there is no infallible assurance that one's prayers help an individual soul in purgatory, or any one of them, here and now. But the mercy and love of God for the souls in purgatory, who are already so close to Him, surely prompt Him to speed their release from the period of purification when the faithful on earth direct their prayers to this purpose."

Thus no genuine assurance is given that the things done in behalf of those believed to be in purgatory really accomplish something. And there is no basis for giving such assurance, for the Bible does not do so. It does not even contain the word "purgatory." The *New Catholic En-*

*cyclopedia* acknowledges: "In the final analysis, the Catholic doctrine on purgatory is based on tradition, not Sacred Scripture."—Vol. 11, p. 1034.

Granted, tradition is not necessarily bad. But this particular tradition is out of harmony with God's Word. The Scriptures do not teach that the "soul" survives the death of the body. Obviously, then, it cannot be subjected to a period of purification in purgatory. Hence, the words of Jesus Christ to the Jewish religious leaders could rightly be directed to those teaching the purgatory doctrine: "You have made the word of God invalid because of your tradition. You hypocrites, Isaiah aptly prophesied about you, when he said, 'This people honors me with their lips, yet their heart is far removed from me. It is in vain that they keep worshiping me, because they teach commands of men as doctrines.' "—Matthew 15:6-9.

Consider also the means for helping those in purgatory, in the light of what is taught in the Holy Scriptures. As noted in the *New Catholic Encyclopedia,* prayer is one of the works of piety that supposedly can help the souls in purgatory. Concerning such prayers, the booklet *Assist the Souls in Purgatory* (published by the Benedictine Convent of Perpetual Adoration) says:

"A short but fervent prayer is often of greater benefit to the poor souls than a prolonged form of devotion which is wanting in attention. Innumerable are the short ejaculatory prayers to which the Church has granted indulgences, all of which are applicable to the poor souls. . . . How easily we can multiply these little fiery darts of prayer during the day as we go from task to task, and even while our hands are busy with some occupation! . . . How many souls could we not relieve or release from purgatory if frequently during the day we offered this short indulgenced prayer of the Church for the departed: 'Eternal rest give unto them, O Lord, and let perpetual light shine upon them. May they rest in peace. Amen.' (Ind[ulgence] of 300 days each time. 'Manual of Indulgences,' 582.) If we repeat with fervent devotion the holy names of 'Jesus, Mary, Joseph' an indulgence of seven years may be gained each time."

Does it not seem strange to you that the repetition of three names would be eight times as effective as a considerably longer, twenty-word prayer? Is repetition of a prayer over and over again what God approves? Concerning this, Jesus Christ said: "When praying, do not say the same things over and over again, just as the people of the nations do, for they imagine they will get a hearing for their use of many words. So, do not make yourselves like them."—Matthew 6:7, 8.

Rather than your saying memorized phrases over and over again, the Bible encourages heartfelt expressions in prayer.

Not to be overlooked is the role that money has had in relation to the purgatory doctrine. Of course, it might be argued that interest in gaining money for the church is not the reason for that teaching. But this does not change the fact that the religious organizations adhering to the purgatory doctrine are pleased to receive material offerings. No one is ever censured by the church for trying to buy his or someone else's way out of purgatory. No one is ever advised by the church that it would be better for him to use his limited material assets for necessities of life. For centuries rich and poor alike have been filling the coffers of religious organizations in the hope of reducing the time they or their loved ones are in purgatory. Observes author Corliss Lamont, in his book *The Illusion of Immortality:*

"The religious ceremonies connected with the departed have meant untold wealth for the Church. Particularly has this been true in the Roman Catholic and Eastern Orthodox faiths where much stress is laid upon masses, prayers and other good offices on behalf of the dead, the dying and all those in any way concerned over their future state.

"Since the early Middle Ages the Catholic Church has obtained, through the granting of indulgences alone, huge sums from rich and poor alike. These indulgences, given in return for money payments, almsgiving or other kinds of offerings, provide that one's own soul or the soul of a deceased relative or friend be spared all or part of its destined punishment in purgatory. . . . In Russia the Orthodox Church accumulated enormous wealth through similar intercessions on behalf of the dead. Besides the steady income from workers and peasants anxious to mitigate divine retribution, many members of the nobility and upper class endowed monasteries and churches on condition that daily prayers be said for their departed souls."

If it were true that such material offerings did benefit the dead, this would mean that God is interested in money. But he does not need anyone's money or material possessions. Speaking through the inspired psalmist, God declares: "I will not take out of your house a bull, out of your pens he-goats. For to me belongs every wild animal of the forest, the beasts upon a thousand mountains. I well know every winged creature of the mountains, and the animal throngs of the open field are with me. If I were hungry, I would not say it to you; for to me the productive land and its fullness belong."—Psalm 50:9-12.

Really, all the riches in the world cannot help a dead man. Money and material possessions cannot even save him from dying. As the Bible says: "Those who are trusting in their means of maintenance, and who keep boasting about the abundance of their riches, not one of them can by any means redeem even a brother, nor give to God a ransom for him; (and the redemption price of their soul is so precious that it has ceased to time indefinite) that he should still live forever and not see the pit."—Psalm 49:6-9.

There can be no question that efforts to help the dead are unscriptural. The teaching that the dead can be aided by the living has only put a heavy burden on people. Knowledge of God's Word, however, frees one from this false idea. This can provide for us real incentive to do our best while our family members are still alive to make them feel that they are needed, loved and appreciated. After their death it is too late for anyone to make up for neglected acts of kindness and consideration.

## CHAPTER 8

# Should You Fear the Dead?

NOT everyone views the dead as the ones who are in need of help. Even more widespread is the belief that the living are the ones who need help—to safeguard them from the dead. At night, cemeteries are often avoided. Strangely, even relatives and friends who were loved while living, after death may come to be viewed as a source of dread and terror.

Among the Indians inhabiting the hills of Central Chiapas, Mexico, red pepper is burned on the day of the burial. This is done in the hope that the unpleasant smoke will drive the soul of the deceased out of the house.

In some parts of Europe, people quickly open all doors and windows as soon as a death occurs. This is done with a view to "liberating" the soul. So that no spell might be cast on anyone, a member of the family places the dead man's hands over his heart and closes the man's eyes with coins.

When a Buddhist of Mongolia dies in a tent, his body is not taken out through the regular opening. Another opening may be made in the tent and, when the body is removed, this opening is closed. Or a masking of straw may be placed in front of the regular door. After the body is carried out, the masking of straw is burned. The purpose of such action is to prevent the spirit of the dead man from coming back into the dwelling and harming the living.

In many parts of Africa, when sickness strikes a family, when a child dies, when a business fails or any other kind of misfortune occurs, a man will quickly consult a juju priest. Usually the priest tells him that a dead family member has been offended. The oracle is consulted and sacrifices are prescribed. The priest charges much money for this and also gets the meat of whatever animal is offered in sacrifice.

Should humans be in such fear of the dead, even going to considerable expense to protect themselves?

The Bible says of the dead: "Their love and their hate and their jealousy have already perished, and they have no portion anymore to time indefinite in anything that has to be done under the sun." (Ecclesiastes 9:6) So there is no harm that can come to you from the dead. And no one can disprove this Bible statement.

True, people may attribute certain manifestations to the spirits of the dead. They may claim that they gained relief from sickness, economic reverses and the like after the spirits of the dead were pacified. But might there not be another source for such trouble and apparent relief from adversity?

Is it not strange that people are unaware of having offended a dead relative until their consulting a juju priest or someone occupying a comparable position? And why should it be that the "spirit" of a dead father, mother, son or daughter would threaten the happiness and welfare of those who, in the past, were deeply loved? What would cause the "spirit" of a dead man to be vengeful when that was not a trait

Fear of the dead moves many to consult juju priests

of the man when alive? Since what is attributed to the deceased is often so contrary to that one's personality when alive, would this not lend strong support to the conclusion that the "spirits" of the dead are not involved? Most assuredly. The Bible is indeed right when it says that the dead have 'no portion in anything that is to be done under the sun.'

Consider also the damaging effect that fear of the dead has on the living. Many have been brought into slavery to juju priests or other religious leaders who claim that the fortunes or misfortunes of a man or woman are largely controlled by the "spirits" of the dead. These men have set themselves up as the ones who can rectify matters with the offended dead. Believing their claims, many people have spent much money on costly ceremonies, money that they might otherwise have used for needed things of life. Even though some maintain that they definitely have been helped through such ceremonies, has their experience produced within them real joy in having had the privilege of doing something to heal a breach with a dead loved one? Rather, do they not act much like a person from whom something has been extorted?

Then, too, think of the deceptive methods that are frequently employed—burning red pepper, taking the deceased through another tent opening and the like—to prevent the "spirit" of the dead from returning and disturbing the living. Would you want to be deceived in this way during your lifetime? Is it reasonable for a person to try to deceive dead persons whom he would never have wanted to deceive while they were alive?

The very practice of resorting to deception can

also have an unwholesome effect on a person. Once a person approves of deceiving the dead whom he views as continuing in conscious existence, will he not weaken his conscience to the point of attempting to deceive the living when that appears to be advantageous?

The One who identifies himself in the Bible as the true God could never approve of the practices that have come about because of people's fear of the dead. Why not? Because those practices, in addition to being based on a false idea, are completely out of harmony with His personality, ways and dealings. "God is not a man that he should tell lies." (Numbers 23:19) He does not approve of deception resorted to for selfish gain. The Bible says: "A man of . . . deception Jehovah detests."—Psalm 5:6.

Since the Bible reveals that the dead are unconscious, why should you fear them? (Psalm 146:4) They can neither help you nor harm you. You now know from the Bible that the "soul" dies and that the "spirit" has no conscious existence apart from the body. Whatever manifestations have given rise to fear of the dead must therefore be from another source. Since in some cases persons claim to gain some improvement in their problems as a result of engaging in acts of appeasement for the dead, this source would have to be one that is willing to bring such temporary relief, but for a wrong motive. What is its aim? To keep people in bondage and blinded to the way to a life free from fear and dread.

It is important to identify this source.

## CHAPTER 9

# Can You Talk with the Dead?

IN LIFE, we humans keenly sense a need to talk with those whom we love. We want to know that our loved ones are well and happy. When things go well for them, we are encouraged. But when we learn that they face grave danger due to a "natural" disaster or some other calamity, we begin to worry. We anxiously wait to hear from them. As soon as we have word that they are safe we are relieved.

The desire to know about the welfare of loved ones has prompted many to want to talk with the dead. They want to know whether their deceased loved ones are happy 'in the beyond.' But is it possible to talk with the dead?

Some maintain that they have periodically felt the presence of a deceased relative or friend and have heard his voice. Others have had like experiences with the help of spirit mediums. Through these mediums they believe that they have heard voices from 'the beyond.' What are they told by such voices? Basically this: 'The dead are very happy and contented. They continue to take a real interest in the life of their surviving loved ones and can see and hear everything they do.'

Regarding such messages, François Grégoire, in his book *L'au-delà* (The Hereafter), observes: "What do these Spirits have to say to us? 'Above all, they appear to be anxious to prove their identity and that they still exist' . . . but on the nature of the other world, nothing essential, not even the smallest revelation."

What do you think about these messages? Do you believe that the dead are actually talking? Since, as the Bible shows, no soul or spirit survives the death of the body to continue conscious existence, could these voices really be the voices of the dead?

## THE CASE OF KING SAUL

Some among those believing that the dead can give messages to the living point to the Holy Bible as confirming their view. One example they cite is an incident involving King Saul of ancient Israel.

Because of his unfaithfulness to Jehovah God, King Saul was cut off from divine direction for carrying out his responsibilities. Therefore, when the Philistines came to wage war against him, in desperation he sought help from a spirit medium. He asked her to bring up the dead prophet Samuel. As to what happened thereafter, the Bible relates:

"When the woman [the medium] saw 'Samuel' she began crying out at the top of her voice; and the woman went on to say to Saul: 'Why did you trick me, when you yourself are Saul?' But the king said to her: 'Do not be afraid, but what did you see?' And the woman went on to say to Saul: 'A god I saw coming up out of the earth.' At once he said to her: 'What is his form?' to which she said: 'It is an old man coming up, and he has himself covered with a sleeveless coat.' At that Saul recognized that it was 'Samuel,' and he proceeded to bow low with his face to the earth and to prostrate himself. And 'Samuel' began to say to Saul: 'Why have you disturbed me by having me brought up?' "—1 Samuel 28:12-15.

Was Saul, in this case, actually brought in touch with the dead prophet Samuel? How could this be, for the Bible links *silence*, not talking, with death? We read: "The dead themselves do not praise Jah [Jehovah], nor do any going down into *silence*."—Psalm 115:17.

Other passages of the Holy Scriptures shed light on the matter. First, it is clear that what Saul did in consulting a spirit medium was a violation of God's law. Both spirit mediums and those consulting them were judged guilty of a capital offense. (Leviticus 20:6, 27) God's law to Israel stated: "Do not turn yourselves to the spirit mediums, and do not consult professional foretellers of events, so as to become unclean by them." (Leviticus 19:31) "When you are entered into the land that Jehovah your God is giving you, you must not learn to do according to the detestable things of those nations. There should not be found in you . . . anyone who consults a spirit medium or a professional foreteller of events or anyone who inquires of the dead."—Deuteronomy 18:9-11; Isaiah 8:19, 20.

If spirit mediums could actually get in touch with the dead, why, then, did God's law label their practice as something "unclean," "detestable" and deserving of death? If the communication were with dead loved ones, for example, why would a God of love designate this as a terrible crime? Why would he want to deprive the living of getting some comforting messages from the dead? Does not God's view indicate that people are not really talking to the dead but that a terrible deception must be involved? Scriptural evidence shows that is the case.

Against this background, consider the case of Saul. Regarding divine communication with him, Saul acknowledged: "God himself has departed from me and has answered me no more, either by means of the prophets or by dreams; so that I am calling you [Samuel] to let me know what I shall do." (1 Samuel 28:15) Obviously, God would not allow a spirit medium to get around this divine cutoff of communication by getting in touch with a dead prophet and having him deliver a message from God to Saul. Then, too, during the latter part of his life, Samuel himself, a faithful prophet of God, had ceased to have any dealings whatsoever with Saul. Would it not be unreasonable, therefore, to conclude that Samuel was willing to speak with Saul by means of a spirit medium, an arrangement that was condemned by God?

Manifestly, there must have been deception involved, something so unclean that spirit mediums

Who was it that spoke to Saul by means of the spirit medium at En-dor?

and those consulting them merited the death sentence. That same deception must be behind claimed communication with the dead today.

Indicating this is the fact that, under the influence of supposed "voices" from the beyond, many persons have committed suicide. They have given up their most precious possession—life—in an effort to join dead loved ones. Others have begun to dread such voices, as the messages have been gloomy, telling of some terrible accident or death about to occur. How could such voices possibly come from a good source? Who or what might be behind these voices?

## CHAPTER 10

# Could It Be a Masterful Deception?

OVER the centuries humans have witnessed the strangest of happenings. Rocks, water glasses and the like have been seen sailing through the air as if moved by invisible hands. Voices, rappings and other noises have been heard even though there was no apparent source or cause for them. Shadowy figures have appeared and then quickly disappeared. At times such happenings have been so well attested to that there is little room for doubt.

Many people consider manifestations of this kind to be evidence that death does not end conscious existence. Some believe that departed spirits are trying in some way to get the attention of the living and to communicate with them.

But one might ask: If these are truly deceased loved ones who are trying to get in touch with the living, why do their manifestations generally frighten observers? What, really, is behind such things?

The Bible clearly shows that death ends all conscious existence. (Ecclesiastes 9:5) Hence, there must be other forces responsible for things that are often attributed to the spirits of the dead. What might those forces be? Could they be intelligent? If so, could they be guilty of perpetrating a masterful deception on humankind?

Surely we do not want to be deceived. To be deceived would mean loss to us and, perhaps, cause us even to come into a position of grave danger. That is why we have good reason to examine the available evidence, reasoning on it, to be sure that we have not fallen victim to a masterful deception. We should be willing to go back as far as possible in human history in an effort to get at the truth of the matter.

The Bible enables us to do that. It takes us back to the time when the first human pair came into existence. In the third chapter of Genesis the Bible relates a conversation that may sound unbelievable to many today. Yet it is not fiction. This conversation provides a clue as to whether a masterful deceiver is at work in human affairs.

### THE START OF DECEPTION

One day, while not in the company of her husband, the first woman, Eve, heard a voice. From all appearances it was the voice of a serpent. Regarding the conversation, the Bible reports:

"Now the serpent proved to be the most cautious

of all the wild beasts of the field that Jehovah God
had made. So it began to say to the woman: 'Is it
really so that God said you must not eat from every
tree of the garden?' At this the woman said to the
serpent: 'Of the fruit of the trees of the garden we
may eat. But as for eating of the fruit of the tree
that is in the middle of the garden, God has said,
"You must not eat from it, no, you must not touch
it that you do not die." ' At this the serpent said to
the woman: 'You positively will not die. For God
knows that in the very day of your eating from it
your eyes are bound to be opened and you are bound
to be like God, knowing good and bad.' Consequently
the woman saw that the tree was good for food
and that it was something to be longed for to the
eyes, yes, the tree was desirable to look upon."
—Genesis 3:1-6.

The message transmitted by the serpent was a
lie. That lie was the first one on record. Accordingly, its source must be the originator or
father of lies. Since the lie led to death-dealing
consequences, the liar was also a murderer. Obviously this liar was not the literal serpent, a
creature that is not endowed with the power of
speech. But there must have been someone behind
the serpent, someone who, by what might be
called ventriloquism, made it appear that the
serpent was talking. That should not seem so
strange to us in this twentieth century when a
cone in the speaker of a radio or a television
set can be made to vibrate in such a way as to
reproduce the human voice. But who was the
speaker behind the serpent?

## AN INVISIBLE DECEIVER

He is identified by Jesus Christ, who himself
had come from the heavens and knew what
went on in the invisible realm. (John 3:13; 8:58)
When certain religious leaders were seeking to

kill him, Jesus said to them: "You are from your father the Devil, and you wish to do the desires of your father. That one was a manslayer when he began, and he did not stand fast in the truth, because truth is not in him. When he speaks the lie, he speaks according to his own disposition, because he is a liar and the father of the lie." —John 8:44.

Being a liar and a manslayer, the Devil is obviously someone who possesses intelligence. This gives rise to the question, How did he come into existence?

The Bible reveals that even before the earth came to be, invisible, spirit persons were enjoying life. Job 38:7 speaks of these spirit persons, "sons of God," as "shouting in applause" when the earth was created. As "sons of God," they received their life from him.—Psalm 90:2.

Hence, the one who deceived Eve by means of the serpent must have been one of these spirit sons, one of God's intelligent creatures. In contradicting God's warning about the tree of the knowledge of good and bad, this one slandered his Creator, making God appear to be a liar. He is therefore rightly called the "Devil," as that word is drawn from the Greek term *di·a'bo·los,* meaning "false accuser, misrepresenter, slanderer." By his course of action this creature set himself in resistance to God and thereby made himself Satan (Hebrew, *sa·tan';* Greek, *sa·ta·nas'*), which means "resister."

Jehovah God cannot be blamed for what this creature did. "Perfect is his activity," says the Bible concerning God, "for all his ways are justice. A God of faithfulness, with whom there is no injustice; righteous and upright is he." (Deuteronomy 32:4) He created his intelligent sons, spirit and human, with the capacity of free will. He did not force them to serve him but wanted them to do so willingly, out of love. He endowed them with the capacity to develop ever greater love for him as their God and Father.

The spirit creature who made himself a resister and a slanderer of God, however, did not choose to perfect his love for his Creator. He allowed selfish ambitions to take root in his heart. (Compare 1 Timothy 3:6.) This is reflected in the conduct of the "king of Tyre" over whom a dirge was rendered in the prophecy of Ezekiel. In the dirge, it is said to the king of Tyre who turned traitor to the kingdom of Israel:

> "You are sealing up a pattern, full of wisdom and perfect in beauty. In Eden, the garden of God, you proved to be. . . . You are the anointed cherub that is covering, and I have set you. On the holy mountain of God you proved to be. In the midst of fiery stones you walked about. You were faultless in your ways from the day of your being created until unrighteousness was found in you. . . . Your heart became haughty because of your beauty. You brought your wisdom to ruin on account of your beaming splendor."—Ezekiel 28:12-17.

The rebellious spirit son of God, similar to the traitorous "king of Tyre," thought too highly of himself. Pride caused him to want to control the human race, and he sought to gain his ends through deception. To this day the majority of humankind are still victims of this deception. By refusing to do God's will as set forth in his Word, the Bible, they actually align themselves with Satan. In so doing, they accept the same lie that Eve did, namely, that choosing to act contrary to God's will can bring real gain.

Since God's Word condemns communication

with the dead, those who try to speak with the dead put themselves on Satan's side. While they may think that they are talking with the dead, they have become the victims of a hoax. Just as Satan made it appear to Eve that a serpent was talking, so he can just as easily make it appear that the dead are talking through mediums. Does this mean that Satan is directly responsible for all the strange phenomena that are often attributed to the spirits of the dead? Or, are others also involved?

## OTHER INVISIBLE DECEIVERS

The Bible reveals that Satan is not the only rebellious spirit creature. Revelation 12:3, 4, 9 shows that there are others. In this Scripture passage Satan the Devil is symbolically depicted as a "great fiery-colored dragon" having a "tail" that "drags a third of the stars of heaven." Yes, Satan was able to use his influence, like a tail, to get other "stars," spirit sons of God, to join him in a rebellious course. (Compare Job 38:7, where spirit sons of God are called "morning stars.") This happened before the global deluge in the days of Noah. Numerous angels, contrary to God's purpose, "forsook their own proper dwelling place" in the heavens, materialized human bodies, lived as husbands with women and fathered hybrid offspring known as Nephilim. Of this, we are told:

'Now it came about that when men started to grow in numbers on the surface of the ground and daughters were born to them, then the sons of the true God began to notice the daughters of men, that they were good-looking; and they went taking wives for themselves, namely, all whom they chose. . . . The Nephilim proved to be in the earth in those days, and also after that, when the sons of the true

God continued to have relations with the daughters of men and they bore sons to them, they were the mighty ones who were of old, the men of fame." —Genesis 6:1-4.

During the Flood these sons of God lost their wives and their hybrid offspring. They themselves had to dematerialize. Respecting what happened to them thereafter, the Bible reports: "God did not hold back from punishing the angels that sinned, but, by throwing them into Tartarus, delivered them to pits of dense darkness to be reserved for judgment." (2 Peter 2:4) And at Jude 6 it adds: "The angels that did not keep their original position but forsook their own proper dwelling place he has reserved with eternal bonds under dense darkness for the judgment of the great day."

As these descriptions relate to spirit creatures, it is evident that the "pits of dense darkness" and "eternal bonds" are not literal. These expressions simply convey to us a picture of restraint, a condition of debasement separated from all divine enlightenment.

There is no Scriptural basis for concluding that these disobedient angels are in a place like the mythological Tartarus of Homer's *Iliad,* that is, in the lowest prison where Cronus and the other Titan spirits were said to be confined. The apostle Peter did not believe in any such mythological gods. So there is no reason to conclude that his use of the Greek expression 'throwing into Tartarus' even hinted at the existence of the mythological place referred to by Homer some nine centuries earlier. In fact, in Greek the expression 'throwing into Tartarus' is only one word, a verb, *tar·ta·ro′o.* It is also used to mean debasing to the lowest degree.

To illustrate, the English word "debase" contains the noun "base." Yet our use of the word does not mean that a *literal base* in some geographical location is involved in the act of debasement. Likewise the Greek verb rendered 'throwing into Tartarus' need not be viewed as suggesting the existence of an actual place, but as suggesting a condition.

At 1 Peter 3:19, 20 the debased spirit creatures are referred to as "spirits in prison, who had once been disobedient when the patience of God was waiting in Noah's days, while the ark was being constructed." Thus the Bible makes it plain that after the Flood the "angels that sinned" came under a form of restraint. There is no Biblical indication that they were able to materialize and take up visible activity on earth after the Flood. So it logically follows that the restraint under which they came made it impossible for them to take on flesh again.

### BEWARE OF DEMON INFLUENCE

It should be noted, however, that the disobedient angels, who now came to be known as demons, had a strong desire to be in close association with humans. They were willing to abandon their heavenly position for the pleasure of living as husbands with women. Scriptural evidence shows that, though restrained from such physical contact now, they have not changed their desires. They seek every means open to them to be in touch with humans and even to control them. Jesus Christ referred to this, using figurative speech in saying:

"When an unclean spirit comes out of a man, it passes through parched places in search of a resting-place, and finds none. Then it says, 'I will go back to my house out of which I moved'; and on arriving it finds it unoccupied but swept clean and adorned. Then it goes its way and takes along with it seven different spirits more wicked than itself, and, after getting inside, they dwell there; and the final circumstances of that man become worse than the first." —Matthew 12:43-45.

It is vital therefore to be on guard lest a person yield himself to demon influence. He may be very uncertain about himself and his future. He may desperately want some assurance that things will go well for him. Or he may find a certain fascination in the weird and frightening manifestations of occult practices. He may hear about someone who reportedly can accurately predict the future. Or he may learn about the various means of divination used—Ouija boards, ESP (extrasensory perception), patterns of tea leaves in cups, oil configurations on water, divining rods, pendulums, the position and movement of stars and planets (astrology), the howling of dogs, the flight of birds, the movement of snakes, crystal-ball gazing and the like. His situation may appear so desperate or his fascination be so great that he may decide to consult a fortune-teller or a medium or to resort to some form of divination. He might be willing to try anything just once.

Is that wise? Definitely not. His curiosity can lead to his coming under demon control. Rather than such a course's bringing him relief and comfort, his situation may only worsen. Supernatural disturbances may rob him of sleep and fill even daylight hours with dread. He may begin to hear strange voices, suggesting that he kill himself or someone else.

Is it not wise therefore to avoid such a risk

and to shun all forms of divination? Je
God does not view this matter lightly. T
tect the Israelites from being deceived and harmed
by wicked spirits, he made the practice of divination a capital offense, saying in the Law: "As for
a man or woman in whom there proves to be a
mediumistic spirit or spirit of prediction, they
should be put to death without fail."—Leviticus
20:27.

God's view of spirit mediums, sorcerers and
divination has not changed. A divine decree still
stands against all practicers of spiritism.—Revelation 21:8.

Therefore exert yourself to resist being deceived by wicked spirit creatures. Should you ever
hear a strange voice, perhaps suggesting that it
is that of a deceased friend or relative, do not
pay any attention. Call upon the name of the
true God, Jehovah, to help you to resist coming
under demon influence. As God's own Son advised,
make your prayerful petition: 'Deliver me from
the wicked one.' (Matthew 6:13) As to items
associated with divination, imitate the example
of those who accepted true worship in ancient
Ephesus. "Quite a number of those who practiced
magical arts [there] brought their books together
and burned them up before everybody." Expensive
as these items were, they did not hold back from
destroying them.—Acts 19:19.

In view of this example, do you think that it
would be right to associate deliberately with
those known to dabble in the occult and to accept
gifts from them? Might they not become the
instrumentalities by means of which you could
come under demon influence?

Our recognizing that wicked spirits are often

responsible for causing people to see or hear weird and frightening manifestations—voices, rappings and shadowy figures for which there are no apparent causes—is a major factor in safeguarding us from being deceived. This knowledge will free us from fearing the dead and from engaging in valueless rites in their behalf. It will also help to prevent our being victimized by wicked spirits.

But if we are to be protected from every aspect of the deception that Satan and his demons have perpetrated in connection with the dead, we must believe and act in harmony with the entire Bible. This is because all of it is the inspired Word of God.

**CHAPTER 11**

# Is Hell Hot?

IS IT NOT a fact that many translations of the Bible refer to a place called "hell"? Yes, many translations of the Holy Scriptures use that expression. But the question is whether the things that the clergy have taught about the place called "hell" have come from the Holy Bible or from some other source.

Did you know that, not only members of Christendom's churches, but many non-Christians as well, have been taught to believe in a hell of torment? It is revealing to read from a variety of sources what is said about the torments of those confined in hell.

A non-Christian "holy book" of the seventh century C.E. says the following:

"Hell!—they will burn therein,—an evil bed (i deed, to lie on)!—Yea, such!—Then shall they taste it,—a boiling fluid, and a fluid dark, murky, intensely cold! . . . (They will be) in the midst of a fierce Blast of Fire and in Boiling Water, and in the shades of Black Smoke: Nothing (will there be) to refresh, nor to please."

Buddhism, which got started in about the sixth century B.C.E., provides this description of one of the "hells" about which it teaches:

"Here there is no interval of cessation either of the flames or of the pain of the beings."

A Roman Catholic *Catechism of Christian Doctrine* (published in 1949) states:

"They are deprived of the vision of God and suffer dreadful torments, especially that of fire, for all eternity. . . . The privation of the beatific vision is called the pain of loss; the torment inflicted by created means on the soul, and on the body after its resurrection, is called the pain of sense."

Also among the Protestant clergy in some places there are those who paint vivid verbal pictures of the horrors of hell. Even their church members at times claim to have had visions of its torments. One man described what he envisioned as follows: 'As far as my eyes could reach there were only burning fire and human beings to be seen. What pain and suffering! Some people screamed, others wailed and begged for water, water! Some rent their hair, others gnashed their teeth; still others bit themselves in the arms and hands.'

The claim is often made that the threatened punishments of hell are a strong force in moving people to do what is right. But do the facts of history bear this out? Have not some of the greatest cruelties been perpetrated by believers in the doctrine of hellfire? Are not the horrible inquisitions and blood-spilling crusades of Christendom examples of this?

So it should come as no surprise that a growing number of people do not really believe in the existence of a hell of torment nor do they view its punishments as a deterrent to wrongdoing. Though not having actually disproved this teaching, they are simply not inclined to believe what does not appeal to them as reasonable and true. Still they may be members of a church that teaches this doctrine and, by supporting it, share responsibility for propagating the teaching of hellfire.

Scenes from Buddhist pictures of hell

But just what does the Bible say about torment after death? If you have read earlier chapters of this book, you know that many common beliefs about the dead are false. You know, according to the Bible, that no soul or spirit separates from the body at death and continues conscious existence. Hence, there is no Scriptural foundation for the doctrine of eternal torment after death, for nothing survives that can be subjected to literal torment. What, then, is the place that various Bible translations refer to as "hell"?

Scenes from the "Inferno" of Catholic Dante

### "SHEOL" IDENTIFIED

In the Catholic *Douay Version,* the first mention of "hell" is found at Genesis 37:35, which quotes the patriarch Jacob as saying respecting Joseph, whom he believed to be dead: "I will go down to my son into hell, mourning." Clearly Jacob was not expressing the idea of joining his son in a place of torment. Even the footnote on this verse in the *Douay Version* (published by the Douay Bible House, New York, 1941) does not put such an interpretation on the text. It says:

"*Into hell.* That is, into *limbo,* the place where the souls of the just were received before the death of our Redeemer. . . . [It] certainly meant the place of rest where he believed his soul to be."

However, nowhere does the Bible itself refer to such a place as "limbo." Nor does it support the idea of a special resting-place for the soul as something distinctly separate from the body. As acknowledged in the glossary of a modern Catholic translation, *The New American Bible* (published by P. J. Kenedy & Sons, New York, 1970): "There is no opposition or difference between soul and body; they are merely different ways of describing the one, concrete reality."

What, then, is the "hell" in which Jacob thought he would join his son? The correct answer to this question lies in getting the proper sense of the original-language word for "hell," namely, *she'ohl'*, which is transliterated "Sheol." This term, also translated as "grave," "pit," "abode of the dead" and "nether world," appears sixty-six times* (in the *New World Translation*) in the thirty-nine books of the Hebrew Scriptures (commonly called the "Old Testament"), but it is never associated with life, activity or torment. To the contrary, it is often linked with death and inactivity. A few examples are:

"For in death there is no mention of you [Jehovah]; in Sheol [the grave, *Authorized Version;* hell, *Douay Version*] who will laud you?"—Psalm 6:5 (6:6, *Douay Version*).

* Genesis 37:35; 42:38; 44:29, 31; Numbers 16:30, 33; Deuteronomy 32:22; 1 Samuel 2:6; 2 Samuel 22:6; 1 Kings 2:6, 9; Job 7:9; 11:8; 14:13; 17:13, 16; 21:13; 24:19; 26:6; Psalms 6:5; 9:17; 16:10; 18:5; 30:3; 31:17; 49:14, 15; 55:15; 86:13; 88:3; 89:48; 116:3; 139:8; 141:7; Proverbs 1:12; 5:5; 7:27; 9:18; 15:11, 24; 23:14; 27:20; 30:16; Ecclesiastes 9:10; Song of Solomon 8:6; Isaiah 5:14; 7:11; 14:9, 11, 15; 28:15, 18; 38:10, 18; 57:9; Ezekiel 31:15-17; 32:21, 27; Hosea 13:14; Amos 9:2; Jonah 2:2; Habakkuk 2:5.

"All that your hand finds to do, do with your very power, for there is no work nor devising nor knowledge nor wisdom in Sheol [the grave, *Authorized Version;* hell, *Douay Version*], the place to which you are going."—Ecclesiastes 9:10.

"For it is not Sheol [the grave, *Authorized Version;* hell, *Douay Version*] that can laud you [Jehovah]; death itself cannot praise you. Those going down into the pit cannot look hopefully to your trueness. The living, the living, he is the one that can laud you, just as I can this day."—Isaiah 38:18, 19.

Hence, Sheol is obviously the place to which the dead go. It is not an individual grave but the common grave of dead mankind in general, where all conscious activity ceases. This is also what the *New Catholic Encyclopedia* acknowledges to be the Biblical significance of Sheol, saying:

"In the Bible it designates the place of complete inertia that one goes down to when one dies whether one be just or wicked, rich or poor." —Vol. 13, p. 170.

That no place of fiery torment existed during the entire Hebrew Scripture period is also confirmed by the fact that torment is never set forth as the penalty for disobedience. The choice that was put before the nation of Israel was, not life or torment, but life or death. Moses told the nation: "I have put life and death before you, the blessing and the malediction; and you must choose life in order that you may keep alive, you and your offspring, by loving Jehovah your God, by listening to his voice and by sticking to him."—Deuteronomy 30:19, 20.

Similarly, God's later appeals for unfaithful Israelites to repent served to encourage them to avoid experiencing, not torment, but an untimely death. Through his prophet Ezekiel, Jehovah declared: "I take delight, not in the death of the wicked one, but in that someone wicked turns back from his way and actually keeps living. Turn back, turn back from your bad ways, for why is it that you should die, O house of Israel?"—Ezekiel 33:11.

## HADES THE SAME AS SHEOL

Yet someone might ask, Did not the coming of Jesus Christ to this earth change matters? No, God does not change his personality or his righteous standards. By means of his prophet Malachi, he stated: "I am Jehovah; I have not changed." (Malachi 3:6) Jehovah has not changed the penalty for disobedience. He is patient with people so that they might be able to escape, not torment, but destruction. As the apostle Peter wrote to fellow believers: "Jehovah is not slow respecting his promise, as some people consider slowness, but he is patient with you because he does not desire any to be destroyed but desires all to attain to repentance."—2 Peter 3:9.

In keeping with the fact that the penalty for disobedience has continued to be death, the place to which the Christian Greek Scriptures (commonly called the "New Testament") describe the dead as going does not differ from the Sheol of the Hebrew Scriptures. (Romans 6:23) This is evident from a comparison of the Hebrew Scriptures with the Christian Greek Scriptures. In its ten occurrences, the Greek word *hai'des,* which is transliterated "Hades," basically conveys the same meaning as the Hebrew word *she'ohl'.* (Matthew 11:23; 16:18; Luke 10:15; 16:23;*
Acts 2:27, 31; Revelation 1:18; 6:8; 20:13, 14

---

* Luke 16:23 is discussed in detail in the next chapter.

[If the translation you are using does not read "hell" or "Hades" in all these texts, you will, nevertheless, note that the terms used instead give no hint of a place of torment.]) Consider the following example:

At Psalm 16:10 (15:10, *Douay Version*) we read: "For you [Jehovah] will not leave my soul in Sheol [hell]. You will not allow your loyal one to see the pit." In a discourse given by the apostle Peter, this psalm was shown to have a prophetic application. Said Peter: "Because [David] was a prophet and knew that God had sworn to him with an oath that he would seat one from the fruitage of his loins upon his throne, he saw beforehand and spoke concerning the resurrection of the Christ, that neither was he forsaken in Hades [hell] nor did his flesh see corruption." (Acts 2:30, 31) Note that the Greek word *hai'des* was used for the Hebrew word *she'ohl'*. Thus Sheol and Hades are seen to be corresponding terms.

Observes the glossary of the French Bible Society's *Nouvelle Version,* under the expression "Abode of the dead":

"This expression translates the Greek word *Hades,* which corresponds to the Hebrew *Sheol.* It is the place where the dead are located between [the time of] their decease and their resurrection (Luke 16:23; Acts 2:27, 31; Rev. 20:13, 14). Certain translations have wrongly rendered this word as *hell.*"

## THE SOURCE OF THE HELLFIRE TEACHING

Clearly, references to Sheol and Hades in the Scriptures do not support the doctrine of a fiery hell. Admitting that it is not Christian and even contradicts the spirit of Christianity, the Catholic periodical *Commonweal* (January 15, 1971) notes:

"For many people, some philosophers included, hell answers a need of the human imagination—a sort of Santa Claus in reverse. . . . Who among the righteous doesn't like to see the unjust get punished with some equity? And if not in this life, why not in the next? Such a view, however, is not compatible with the New Testament, which invites man to life and to love."

Then this magazine goes on to show probable sources of this doctrine, saying:

"Another element that might have contributed to the traditional Christian concept of hell can be found in the Roman world. Just as intrinsic immortality was a premise in a major part of Greek philosophy, justice was a primary virtue among the Romans, particularly when Christianity began to thrive. . . . The wedding of these two minds—the philosophical Greek and judicial Roman—might well have brought about the theological symmetry of heaven and hell: if the good soul is rewarded, then the bad soul is punished. To confirm their belief in justice for the unjust, the Romans merely had to pick up Virgil's *Aeneid* and read about the blessed in Elysium and the damned in Tartarus, which was surrounded by fire and overflowing with the panic of punishment."

The teaching about a fiery hell is thus acknowledged to be a belief shared by persons alienated from God. It can rightly be designated as a 'teaching of demons.' (1 Timothy 4:1) This is so because it has its source in the falsehood that man does not really die, and it mirrors the morbid, vicious and cruel disposition of the demons. (Compare Mark 5:2-13.) Has not this doctrine needlessly filled people with dread and horror? Has it not grossly misrepresented God? In his Word, Jehovah reveals himself to be a God of love. (1 John 4:8) But the teaching about a fiery hell slanders him, falsely accusing him of the worst cruelties imaginable.

Those teaching the hellfire doctrine are therefore saying blasphemous things against God. While some clergymen may not be familiar with the Biblical evidence, they should be. They represent themselves as speaking God's message and therefore are under obligation to know what the Bible says. They certainly know full well that what they do and say can deeply affect the lives of those who look to them for instruction. That should cause them to be careful in making sure of their teaching. Any misrepresentation of God can turn people away from true worship, to their injury.

There can be no question that Jehovah God does not look with approval upon false teachers. To unfaithful religious leaders of ancient Israel, he pronounced the following judgment: "I . . . for my part, shall certainly make you to be despised and low to all the people, according as you were not keeping my ways." (Malachi 2:9) We can be sure that like judgment will come upon false religious teachers of our time. The Bible indicates that they will soon be stripped of their position and influence by the political elements of the world. (Revelation 17:15-18) As for those who continue to support religious systems teaching lies, they will fare no better. Jesus Christ said: "If . . . a blind man guides a blind man, both will fall into a pit."—Matthew 15:14.

That being the case, would you want to continue supporting any religious system that teaches a fiery hell? How would you feel if your father had been maliciously slandered? Would you continue to accept the slanderers as your friends? Would you not, rather, cut off all association with them? Should we not likewise want to break off all association with those who have slandered our heavenly Father?

Fear of torment is not the proper motivation for serving God. He desires that our worship be motivated by love. This should appeal to our hearts. Our realizing that the dead are not in a place filled with screaming anguish in blazing fires, but, rather, are unconscious in the silent and lifeless common grave of dead mankind can remove a barrier to our expressing such love for God.

## CHAPTER 12

# A Rich Man in Hades

SINCE Hades is just the common grave of dead mankind, why does the Bible speak of a rich man as undergoing torments in the fire of Hades? Does this show that Hades, or at least a part of it, is a place of fiery torment?

Teachers of hellfire eagerly point to this account as definite proof that there is indeed a hell of torment that awaits the wicked. But, in so doing, they disregard such clear and repeated Biblical statements as: "The soul that is sinning —it itself will die." (Ezekiel 18:4, 20) And: "As for the dead, they are conscious of nothing at all." (Ecclesiastes 9:5) Clearly these statements do not support the idea of torment for "lost souls" in a fiery hell.

The Bible's teaching about the condition of the dead therefore leaves many of Christendom's clergymen in an awkward position. The very book on which they claim to base their teachings, the Bible, conflicts with their doctrines. Yet, consciously or subconsciously, they feel impelled to reach into the Bible to seize on something to prove their point, thereby blinding themselves and others to the truth. Often this is done deliberately.

On the other hand, sincere seekers for the truth want to know what is right. They realize that they would only be fooling themselves if they rejected portions of God's Word while claiming to base their beliefs on other parts. They want to know what the Bible actually says about the condition of the dead. And, to fill out the picture, they want to know the meaning of what is said about the rich man who experienced torment in Hades, and how that fits in with the rest of the Bible.

It was Jesus Christ who spoke about a certain rich man and also a beggar named Lazarus. His words are found at Luke 16:19-31 and read:

"A certain man was rich, and he used to deck himself with purple and linen, enjoying himself from day to day with magnificence. But a certain beggar named Lazarus used to be put at his gate, full of ulcers and desiring to be filled with the things dropping from the table of the rich man. Yes, too, the dogs would come and lick his ulcers. Now in course of time the beggar died and he was carried off by the angels to the bosom position of Abraham.

"Also, the rich man died and was buried. And in Hades he lifted up his eyes, he existing in torments, and he saw Abraham afar off and Lazarus in the bosom position with him. So he called and said, 'Father Abraham, have mercy on me and send Lazarus to dip the tip of his finger in water and cool my tongue, because I am in anguish in this blazing fire.' But Abraham said, 'Child, remember that you received in full your good things in your lifetime, but Lazarus correspondingly the injurious things. Now, however, he is having comfort here but you are in anguish. And besides all these things, a great chasm has been fixed between us and you people, so that those wanting to go over from here to you people cannot, neither may people cross over from there to us.' Then he said, 'In that event I ask you, father, to send him to the house of my father, for I have five brothers, in order that he may give them a thorough witness, that they also should not get into this place of torment.' But Abraham said, 'They have Moses and the Prophets; let them listen to these.' Then he said, 'No, indeed, father Abraham, but if someone from the dead goes to them they will repent.' But he said to him, 'If they do not listen to Moses and the Prophets, neither will they be persuaded if someone rises from the dead.' "

Note what is said about the rich man. Why was he tormented in Hades? What had he done? Jesus did not say that the rich man led a degraded life, did he? All that Jesus said was that the man

was rich, dressed well and feasted sumptuously.
Does such conduct of itself merit punishment
by torment? True, a serious failing is implied
in the attitude of the rich man toward the beggar Lazarus. The rich man lacked compassion
for him. But did that failing distinguish him sufficiently from Lazarus?

Think about what Jesus said concerning Lazarus. Is there anything in the account to lead us
to conclude that, if the situation had been re-
versed, Lazarus would have been a compassionate
man? Do we read that Lazarus built up a record
of fine works with God, leading to his coming
into the "bosom position of Abraham," that is,
a position of divine favor? Jesus did not say
that. He merely described Lazarus as a sickly
beggar.

So is it logical to conclude that all sickly beg-
gars will receive divine blessings at death, whereas
all rich men will go to a place of conscious torment? Not at all. Begging is of itself no mark of
God's favor. To the contrary, the Bible contains
the prayerful expression:
"Give me neither poverty
nor riches." (Proverbs
30:8) And of his time,
King David wrote: "I
have not seen
anyone righ-
teous left en-
tirely, nor his
offspring look-
ing for bread."
—Psalm 37:25.

If we take Jesus' words literally, we would have to draw still other conclusions that would make the illustration strange indeed. These include: That those enjoying celestial happiness are in position to see and speak to those suffering torment in Hades. That the water adhering to one's fingertip is not evaporated by the fire of Hades. And, that, although the torment of Hades is great, a mere drop of water would bring relief to the sufferer.

Taken literally, do these things sound reasonable to you? Or, do you feel, instead, that what Jesus said was not meant to be taken literally? Is there any way to be sure?

### THE "RICH MAN" AND "LAZARUS" IDENTIFIED

Examine the context. To whom was Jesus talking? At Luke 16:14 we are told: "Now the Pharisees, who were money lovers, were listening to all these things, and they began to sneer at him."

Since Jesus spoke in the hearing of the Pharisees, was he relating an actual case or was he simply using an illustration? Concerning Jesus' method of teaching the crowds, we read: "Indeed, without an illustration he would not speak to them." (Matthew 13:34) Accordingly, the account about the rich man and Lazarus must be an illustration.

This illustration was evidently directed to the Pharisees. As a class they were like the rich man. They loved money, as well as prominence and flattering titles. Jesus said of them: "All the works they do they do to be viewed by men; for they broaden the scripture-containing cases that they wear as safeguards, and enlarge the fringes of their garments. They like the most prominent place at evening meals and the front seats in the synagogues, and the greetings in the marketplaces and to be called Rabbi by men." —Matthew 23:5-7.

The Pharisees looked down on others, especially on tax collectors, harlots and others having the reputation of being sinners. (Luke 18:11, 12) On one occasion when officers, sent to arrest Jesus, came back empty-handed because of having been impressed by his teaching, the Pharisees spoke up: "You have not been misled also, have you? Not one of the rulers or of the Pharisees has put faith in him, has he? But this crowd that does not know the Law are accursed people." —John 7:47-49.

Hence, in the parable the beggar Lazarus well represents those humble persons whom the Pharisees despised but who repented and became followers of Jesus Christ. Jesus showed that these despised sinners, upon repenting, would gain a position of divine favor, whereas the Pharisees and other prominent religious leaders as a class would lose out. He said: "Truly I say to you that the tax collectors and the harlots are going ahead of you into the kingdom of God. For John came to you in a way of righteousness, but you did not believe him. However, the tax collectors and the harlots believed him, and you, although you saw this, did not feel regret afterwards so as to believe him."—Matthew 21:31, 32.

### DEATH OF THE "RICH MAN" AND OF "LAZARUS"

What, then, is signified by the death of the "rich man" and of "Lazarus"? We do not need to conclude that it refers to actual death. As used in the Bible, death can also represent a great change in the condition of individuals. For example: Persons pursuing a course of life contrary to God's will are spoken of as being 'dead in trespasses and sins.' But when they come into an approved standing before God as disciples of Jesus Christ they are referred to as coming "alive." (Ephesians 2:1, 5; Colossians 2:13) At the same time such living persons become "dead" to sin. We read: "Reckon yourselves to be dead indeed with reference to sin but living with reference to God by Christ Jesus."—Romans 6:11.

Since both the "rich man" and "Lazarus" of Jesus' parable are clearly symbolic, logically their deaths are also symbolic. But in what sense do they die?

The key to answering this question lies in what Jesus said just before introducing the illustration: "Everyone that divorces his wife and marries another commits adultery, and he that marries a woman divorced from a husband commits adultery." (Luke 16:18) This statement may appear to be completely unrelated to the illustration. But this is not the case.

By reason of the Mosaic law the nation of Israel was in a covenant relationship with God and therefore could be spoken of as being a wife to him. At Jeremiah 3:14, for example, God refers to the nation as an unfaithful wife: " 'Return, O you renegade sons,' is the utterance of Jehovah. 'For I myself have become the husbandly owner of you people.' " Then, with the coming of Jesus, an opportunity was extended to the Jews to become part of his "bride." That is why John the Baptist said to his disciples: "You yourselves bear me witness that I said, I am not the Christ, but, I have been sent forth in advance of that one. He that has the bride is the bridegroom. However, the friend of the bridegroom, when he stands and hears him, has a great deal of joy on account of the voice of the bridegroom. Therefore this joy of mine has been made full. That one [Jesus] must go on increasing, but I must go on decreasing."—John 3:28-30.

In order to become part of Christ's "bride," the Jews had to be released from the Law that made them, figuratively speaking, a wife to God. Without such release, they could not come into a wifely relationship with Christ, as that would be an adulterous relationship. The words of Romans 7:1-6 confirm this:

> "Can it be that you do not know, brothers, (for I am speaking to those who know law,) that the Law is master over a man as long as he lives? For instance, a married woman is bound by law to her husband while he is alive; but if her husband dies, she is discharged from the law of her husband. So, then, while her husband is living, she would be styled an adulteress if she became another man's. But if her husband dies, she is free from his law, so that she is not an adulteress if she becomes another man's.

> "So, my brothers, *you also were made dead to the Law* through the body of the Christ, that you might become another's, the one's who was raised up from the dead, that we should bear fruit to God. . . . Now we have been discharged from the Law, because we have died to that by which we were being held fast, that we might be slaves in a new sense by the spirit, and not in the old sense by the written code."

While the death of Jesus Christ was the basis for releasing the Jews from the Law, even before his death repentant ones could come into a favored position with God as disciples of his Son.

The message and work of John the Baptist and of Jesus Christ opened the door for the Jews to seize the opportunity to gain divine favor and put themselves in line for a heavenly inheritance as members of Christ's bride. As Jesus himself expressed it: "From the days of John the Baptist until now the kingdom of the heavens is the goal toward which men press, and those pressing forward are seizing it."—Matthew 11:12.

Hence, the work and message of John the Baptist and of Jesus Christ began to lead toward a complete change in the condition of the symbolic "rich man" and "Lazarus." Both classes died to their former condition. The repentant "Lazarus" class came into a position of divine favor, whereas the "rich man" class came under divine disfavor because of persisting in unrepentance. At one time the "Lazarus" class had looked to the Pharisees and other religious leaders of Judaism for spiritual "crumbs." But Jesus' imparting the truth to them filled their spiritual needs. Contrasting the spiritual feeding provided by Jesus with that of the religious leaders, the Bible reports: "The crowds were astounded at his way of teaching; for he was teaching them as a person having authority, and not as their scribes." (Matthew 7:28, 29) Truly a complete reversal had taken place. The religious leaders of Judaism were shown up as having nothing to offer to the "Lazarus" class.

On the day of Pentecost of the year 33 C.E. the change in conditions was accomplished. At that time the new covenant replaced the old Law covenant. Those who had repented and accepted Jesus were then fully released from the old Law covenant. They died to it. On that day of Pentecost there was also unmistakable evidence that the disciples of Jesus Christ had been exalted far above the Pharisees and other prominent religious leaders. Not the religious leaders of Judaism, but these disciples received God's spirit, enabling them to speak about "the magnificent things of God" in the native languages of people from widely scattered places. (Acts 2:5-11) What a marvelous manifestation this was of their having God's blessing and approval! The "Lazarus" class had indeed come into the favored situation by becoming the spiritual seed of the Greater Abraham, Jehovah. This was pictured as the "bosom position."—Compare John 1:18.

As for the unrepentant Pharisees and other prominent religious leaders, they were dead to their former position of seeming favor. They were in "Hades." Remaining unrepentant, they were separated from the faithful disciples of Jesus as if by a "great chasm." This was a "chasm" of God's unchangeable, righteous judgment. Of this, we read in Scripture: "Your judicial decision is a vast watery deep."—Psalm 36:6.

## THE "RICH MAN'S" TORMENT

The "rich man" class was also tormented. How? By the fiery judgment messages of God being proclaimed by Jesus' disciples.—Compare Revelation 14:10.

That the religious leaders were tormented by the message proclaimed by Jesus' disciples there can be no question. They tried desperately to stop the proclamation. When the apostles of Jesus Christ made their defense before the Jewish supreme court composed of prominent religious men, the judges "felt deeply cut and were wanting to do away with them." (Acts 5:33) Later, the disciple Stephen's defense had a like tormenting effect upon the members of that court. "They felt cut to their hearts and began to gnash their teeth at him."—Acts 7:54.

These religious leaders wanted the disciples of Jesus to come and 'cool their tongue.' They wanted the "Lazarus" class to leave the "bosom position" of God's favor and present his message in such a way as not to cause them discomfort. Similarly, they wanted the "Lazarus" class to water down God's message so as not to put their "five brothers," their religious allies, in a "place of torment." Yes, they did not want any of their associates to be tormented by judgment messages.

But, as indicated by Jesus' illustration, neither the "rich man" class nor his religious allies would be freed from the tormenting effects of the message proclaimed by the "Lazarus" class. The apostles of the Lord Jesus Christ refused to water down the message. They refused to stop teaching on the basis of Jesus' name. Their reply to the Jewish supreme court was: "We must obey God as ruler rather than men."—Acts 5:29.

If the religious allies of the "rich man" wanted to escape that torment, they could do so. They had "Moses and the Prophets," that is, they had the inspired Holy Scriptures written by Moses and other ancient prophets. Not once did those inspired Scriptures point to any literal place of torment after death, but they did contain all that was necessary to identify Jesus as the promised Messiah or Christ. (Deuteronomy 18:15, 18, 19; 1 Peter 1:10, 11) Hence, if the "rich man" class and his "five brothers" had paid attention to "Moses and the Prophets," they would have accepted Jesus as the Messiah. That would have brought them in line for divine favor and shielded them from the tormenting effects of God's judgment message.

## CHRISTENDOM SHOULD KNOW

There is little reason for Christendom's clergymen not to be familiar with this understanding of Jesus' parable. A leading Protestant commentary, *The Interpreter's Bible,* calls attention to a similar explanation. It points out that many interpreters believe Jesus' words to be "an allegorical appendix that presupposes the conflict between early Christianity and orthodox Judaism. The rich man and his brothers represent the unbelieving Jews. Jesus is made to assert that they have stubbornly refused to repent in spite of the obvious testimony to himself in Scripture and to predict that they will fail to be impressed by his resurrection. It is conceivable that Luke and his readers imposed some such interpretation on these verses." And, in a footnote on Luke chapter 16, the Catholic *Jerusalem Bible* acknowledges that this is a "parable in story form without reference to any historical personage."

In view of this, we can rightly ask: Why have Christendom's clergymen not at least acknowledged to their church people that this is a parable? Why do those who know that the Bible does not teach the immortality of the human soul continue to put a literal application on an obvious parable? Is this not dishonest? Are they not showing disregard for the Word of God, deliberately hiding the facts?

The illustration of the rich man and Lazarus contains vital lessons for us today. Are we paying attention to the inspired Word of God? Do we desire to follow it as devoted disciples of Jesus Christ? Those who refuse to do so, like the Jewish Pharisees, will not escape the tormenting effects of God's judgment message against them. His loyal servants will keep right on declaring the truth, fearlessly exposing religious error.

Where do you stand in this matter? Do you believe there should be a letup on such an exposure, feeling that there is good in all religions? Or, do you feel indignant about Christendom's misrepresenting God by its false doctrines about the dead? Do you want to see God's name cleared of the reproach brought upon it through the teaching of false doctrines? Do you desire to see no effort spared in freeing honest-hearted ones from bondage to religious falsehoods? If you do, you will find God's purpose concerning the dead and the living most comforting.

## CHAPTER 13

# What About the Fire of Gehenna?

'GRANTED,' someone might say, 'Hades is never used in the Bible to refer to a place of fiery torment. But does not the Bible speak of "hell fire"?'

True, numerous translations of the Christian Greek Scriptures (commonly called the "New Testament") use the expression "hell fire" or "fires of hell." In this case the Greek term rendered "hell" is *ge'en·na* (Gehenna). But is Gehenna the name of a place of fiery torment? Yes, say many of Christendom's commentators. Yet they well know that the soul is not immortal. They also know that the Scriptures show that immortality is bestowed as a reward only upon those whom God designates as worthy of receiving it, and not as a curse on the wicked so that they might be tormented everlastingly.—Romans 2:6, 7; 1 Corinthians 15:53, 54.

Other commentators of Christendom acknowledge that Gehenna is not a place of eternal fiery torment. Says *The New Bible Commentary* (page 779): "Gehenna was the Hellenized form of the name of the valley of Hinnom at Jerusalem in which fires were kept constantly burning to consume the refuse of the city. This is a powerful picture of final destruction."

What is the truth of the matter? The best way to find out is to examine what the Bible itself says.

The term "Gehenna" is found twelve times in the Christian Greek Scriptures. Once it is used by the disciple James, and eleven times it appears in statements attributed to Jesus Christ and relates to a condemnatory judgment. These texts read:

"I say to you that everyone who continues wrathful with his brother will be accountable to the court of justice; but whoever addresses his brother with an unspeakable word of contempt will be accountable to the Supreme Court; whereas whoever says, 'You despicable fool!' [thereby wrongly judging and condemning his brother as morally worthless] will be liable to the fiery Gehenna."—Matthew 5:22.

"Do not become fearful of those who kill the body but cannot kill the soul; but rather be in fear of him that can destroy both soul and body in Gehenna." —Matthew 10:28.

"I will indicate to you whom to fear: Fear him who after killing has authority to throw into Gehenna. Yes, I tell you, fear this One."—Luke 12:5.

"Woe to you, scribes and Pharisees, hypocrites! because you traverse sea and dry land to make one proselyte, and when he becomes one you make him a subject for Gehenna twice as much so as yourselves. Serpents, offspring of vipers, how are you to flee from the judgment of Gehenna?"—Matthew 23:15, 33.

"If ever your hand makes you stumble, cut it off; it is finer for you to enter into life maimed than with two hands to go off into Gehenna, into the fire that cannot be put out. And if your foot makes you stumble, cut it off; it is finer for you to enter into life lame than with two feet to be pitched into Gehenna. And if your eye makes you stumble, throw it away; it is finer for you to enter one-eyed into the kingdom of God than with two eyes to be pitched into Gehenna, where their maggot does not die and the fire is not put out."—Mark 9:43-48; see also the similarly worded passages at Matthew 5:29, 30; 18:8, 9.

"Well, the tongue is a fire. The tongue is constituted a world of unrighteousness among our members, for it spots up all the body and sets the wheel of natural life aflame and it is set aflame by Gehenna [that is, improper use of the tongue is as destructive as Gehenna; it can so affect the whole round of life into which a person comes by birth that it can lead to his meriting the judgment of Gehenna]."—James 3:6.

Note that, while these texts associate fire with Gehenna, none of them speak of any conscious existence, any suffering, after death. Rather, as shown at Matthew 10:28, Jesus pointed out that God can "destroy," not merely the body, but the entire person, the soul, in Gehenna. Just what is the nature of this destruction? An understanding of this is gleaned from a closer examination of the word "Gehenna."

## GEHENNA—THE VALLEY OF HINNOM

Though found in the Christian Greek Scriptures, "Gehenna" is drawn from two Hebrew words, *Ga'i* and *Hin·nom'*, meaning Valley of Hinnom. This valley lay south and southwest of Jerusalem. In the days of faithless Judean Kings Ahaz and Manasseh the Valley of Hinnom served as a place for idolatrous religious rites, including the abhorrent practice of child sacrifice. (2 Chronicles 28:1, 3; 33:1, 6; Jeremiah 7:31; 19:2, 6) Later, good King Josiah put a stop to the idolatrous worship carried on there and made the valley unfit to use for worship.—2 Kings 23:10.

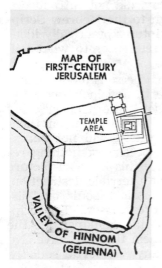

MAP OF FIRST-CENTURY JERUSALEM

TEMPLE AREA

VALLEY OF HINNOM (GEHENNA)

Tradition relates that the Valley of Hinnom thereafter became a place for the disposal of garbage. And the Bible provides confirmation for this. At Jeremiah 31:40, for example, the Valley of Hinnom is evidently called the "low plain of the carcasses and of the fatty ashes." There was also the "Gate of the Ash-heaps," a gate that seems to have opened out onto the eastern extremity of the Valley of Hinnom at its juncture with the Kidron Valley.—Nehemiah 3:13, 14.

That Gehenna should be linked with the destructive aspects of a city dump is in full agreement with the words of Jesus Christ. With reference to Gehenna, he said, "their maggot does not die and the fire is not put out." (Mark 9:48) His words evidently allude to the fact that fires burned continually at the city dump, perhaps being intensified by the addition of sulfur. Where the fire did not reach, worms or maggots would breed and feed on what was not consumed by fire.

It should also be observed that Jesus, in speaking of Gehenna in this way, did not introduce a concept completely foreign to the Hebrew Scriptures. In those earlier Scriptures practically identical wording appears in references to what will befall the ungodly.

Isaiah 66:24 foretells that persons having God's favor "will actually go forth and look upon the carcasses of the men that were transgressing against [God]; for the very worms upon them will not die and their fire itself will not be extinguished, and they must become something repulsive to all flesh." Clearly this is not a picture of conscious torment but of a terrible destruction. What are left are, not conscious souls or "disembodied spirits," but dead "carcasses." The scripture shows that it is, not the humans, but the maggots or worms upon them that are alive. No mention is made here of any "immortal soul."

In the prophecy of Jeremiah the Valley of Hinnom is similarly linked with a destruction of faithless humans. " 'Look! there are days coming,' is the utterance of Jehovah, 'when this place will be called no more Topheth and the valley of the son of Hinnom, but the valley of the killing. And I will make void the counsel of Judah and of Jerusalem in this place, and I will cause them to fall by the sword before their enemies and by the hand of those seeking for their soul. And I will give their dead bodies as food to the flying creatures of the heavens and to the beasts of the earth.' "—Jeremiah 19:6, 7.

Note that Jeremiah's reference to the Valley of Hinnom contains no hint of conscious torment after death. The picture drawn is one of total destruction, the "dead bodies" being consumed by scavenger birds and beasts.

## A SYMBOL OF DESTRUCTION

In keeping with the Biblical evidence, then, Gehenna or the Valley of Hinnom could appropriately serve as a symbol of destruction but not of conscious fiery torment. Joseph E. Kokjohn, in the Catholic periodical *Commonweal,* acknowledges this, saying:

> "The final place of punishment, evidently, is Gehenna, the Valley of Hinno[m], which at one time had been a place where human sacrifice was offered to pagan gods, but in biblical times had already become the city dump, a refuse heap on the outskirts of Jerusalem. Here the stench and smoke and fire were a constant reminder to the inhabitants of what happened to things that had served their purpose—they were destroyed."

That the destruction symbolized by Gehenna is a lasting one is shown elsewhere in the Holy Scriptures. The apostle Paul, when writing to Christians at Thessalonica, said that those causing them tribulation would "undergo the judicial punishment of *everlasting destruction* from before the Lord and from the glory of his strength." —2 Thessalonians 1:6-9.

Biblical evidence thus makes it plain that those whom God judges as undeserving of life will experience, not eternal torment in a literal fire, but "everlasting destruction." They will not be preserved alive anywhere. The fire of Gehenna is therefore but a symbol of the totality and thoroughness of that destruction.

It is noteworthy that, in addressing the religious leaders of his day, Jesus Christ said: "Serpents, offspring of vipers, how are you to flee from the judgment of Gehenna?" (Matthew 23:33) Why was this? It was because those religious leaders were hypocrites. They desired to be looked up to and addressed with high-sounding titles, but they had no regard for those whom they were to help spiritually. They burdened others down with traditional regulations, and disregarded justice, mercy and faithfulness. They were false teachers, placing human traditions above the authority of God's Word.—Matthew 15:3-6; 23:1-32.

Have you noticed like things among the religious leaders of today, particularly in Christendom? Will they fare any better than the religious leaders of Judaism in the days of Jesus' earthly ministry? Not in the least, for Christendom's religious leaders have disobediently misrepresented God and the "good news about our Lord Jesus." So as long as they persist in teaching false doctrines they stand in danger of undergoing the "judicial punishment of everlasting destruction."

The truth about Gehenna therefore should help us to appreciate the importance of avoiding association with false religion. Not only the leaders but, as Jesus showed, also those who support the false religious teachers are in danger. Jesus Christ, in fact, spoke of a proselyte of the scribes and Pharisees as becoming a 'subject for Gehenna twice as much so as they were.' (Matthew 23:

15) Hence, people who blindly continue to follow false religious teaching today cannot hope to escape God's adverse judgment.

While making us think seriously about our own position, this can also be a comforting assurance to us. How so? In that we can be sure that Jehovah God will not leave serious wrongdoing unpunished. If people do not want to conform to his righteous laws and deliberately persist in a course of wickedness, he will not allow them much longer to continue to disrupt the peace of righteous people.

## CHAPTER 14

# What 'Torment in the Lake of Fire' Means

HOW would you react if, now that you know what the Bible says about the unconscious condition of the dead, you were to find a Bible text mentioning a place of torment? Would you reason that this justifies ignoring all the other scriptures and holding onto the idea that there may still be a possibility of conscious existence continuing after death? Or, would you undertake a careful examination of the context to determine just what the text might really mean and how it harmonizes with the rest of the Bible?

The reason for considering this is that the Bible book of Revelation does speak of "torment" in a "lake of fire." Revelation 20:10 states: "The Devil who was misleading them was hurled into the lake of fire and sulphur, where both the wild beast and the false prophet already were; and they will be tormented day and night forever and ever."—See also Revelation 19:20.

How are those cast into the "lake of fire" tormented? That we should not be hasty in taking this expression as literal is evident from the nature of the book of Revelation. The opening ·words of the book read: "A revelation by Jesus Christ, which God gave him, to show his slaves the things that must shortly take place. And he sent forth his angel and presented it in signs through him to his slave John."—Revelation 1:1.

As there stated, this revelation was presented "in signs." What, then, of the "lake of fire" and the "torment" there? Are they literal or are they also "signs" or symbols?

Additional information as to what is cast into the lake of fire, besides the Devil, the "wild beast" and the "false prophet," sheds light on the matter. Note the words of Revelation 20:14, 15: "Death and Hades were hurled into the lake of fire. This means the second death, the lake of fire. Furthermore, whoever was not found written in the book of life was hurled into the lake of fire."

Now, is it possible for death and Hades to be hurled into a literal lake of fire? Obviously not, for they are not objects, animals or persons. Death is a state or condition. How could it be tossed into a literal lake of fire? As for Hades, it is the common grave of mankind. What kind of a lake could hold it?

Then, too, Revelation 20:14, 15 does not say that the lake is literal. Rather, we read that the "lake of fire" is itself a sign or symbol of "second death." The same point is made at Revelation 21:8: "As for the cowards and those without faith and those who are disgusting in their filth and murderers and fornicators and those practicing spiritism and idolaters and all the liars, their portion will be in the lake that burns with fire and sulphur. *This means the second death.*"

Since the lake of fire is a symbol of second death, the casting of death and Hades into it is simply a symbolic way of saying that these will be forever destroyed. This agrees with the Bible's statement that 'the last enemy, death, is to be brought to nothing.' (1 Corinthians 15:26) And, since Hades, the common grave of mankind in general, is emptied and "death will be no more," that means that Hades ceases to function, passes out of existence.—Revelation 20:13; 21:4.

### FIGURATIVE TORMENT

What, then, is the "torment" experienced by wicked humans and others that are thrown into the "lake of fire"? Without conscious existence, they could not experience *literal* torment, could they? And there is nothing in the Holy Scriptures to show that they will have any conscious existence. So why does the Bible speak of eternal torment in the "lake of fire"?

Since the "lake of fire" is symbolic, the torment associated with it must also be symbolic or figurative. This can be better appreciated in the light of what the Bible says about Jesus' being released from the grip of death. We read: "God resurrected him by loosing the pangs of death, because it was not possible for him to continue to be held fast by it." (Acts 2:24) Certainly Jesus was not suffering conscious torment while dead. What "pangs," then, did he experience? He was held by figurative restraining bonds. Speaking of these, the psalmist describes the threat of death that faced him as follows: "The ropes of death encircled me and the distressing circumstances of Sheol themselves found me."—Psalm 116:3.

Thus the effects of death are comparable to one's being tied up with ropes in total restraint. Death, in fact, results in the greatest restraint possible, ending all activity and thought processes. Hence, the deceased, though unconscious, is spoken of in the Scriptures as being subject to its "pangs" or pains.

Even more appropriately, then, those who experience "second death" (as symbolized by the lake of fire) may be said to undergo a figurative torment, one that lasts forever. This is because there is no release from the restraint of second death. Since second death keeps hold of them, they are "tormented" forever in the sense of being eternally restrained from having any conscious existence or activity. That their restraint in "second death" is compared to torture by being confined in prison is shown by Jesus in his parable of the ungrateful, merciless slave. Concerning the action his master took against him, Jesus said: "And in his anger the master handed him over to the torturers till he should pay all his debt." (Matthew 18:34, *Jerusalem Bible*) The *New World Translation* shows who these tormentors are by reading: "With that his master, provoked to wrath, delivered him to the jailers [*marginal reading:* tormentors], until he should pay back all that was owing."

The very fact that the "lake of fire" is a symbol

of "second death" rules out the idea of its being a place of conscious torment. Nowhere does the Bible even suggest that the dead can experience conscious torment, but the dead have lost all sensations. Of those dead in the common grave of mankind, the Bible says: "There the wicked themselves have ceased from agitation, and there those weary in power are at rest. Together prisoners themselves are at ease; they actually do not hear the voice of one driving them to work. Small and great are there the same, and the slave is set free from his master."—Job 3:17-19.

Just as the death to which humans in general continue to be subject ends all sensations and feelings, so does "second death." At the same time both deaths are rightly linked with figurative pangs or torment, because of the unpleasant, total restraint under which they bring the individual.

Yet even before wicked ones are plunged into total annihilation, "second death," they experience torment. This is referred to symbolically at Revelation 14:9-11: "If anyone worships the wild beast and its image, and receives a mark on his forehead or upon his hand, he will also drink of the wine of the anger of God that is poured out undiluted into the cup of his wrath, and he shall be tormented with fire and sulphur in the sight of the holy angels and in the sight of the Lamb. And the smoke of their torment ascends forever and ever, and day and night they have no rest, those who worship the wild beast and its image, and whoever receives the mark of its name." By what means are the worshipers of the "wild beast" and its "image" tormented? The words of Revelation that follow immediately thereafter provide the clue: "Here is where it means endurance for the holy ones, those who observe the commandments of God and the faith of Jesus."—Revelation 14:12.

There would be no need for endurance on the part of the holy ones if the worshipers of the "wild beast" and its "image" were confined to a literal place of torment. Those false worshipers would then be stripped of all power to do harm to God's faithful servants. But as long as they are alive and free they can engage in hateful, vicious acts against the "holy ones."

The fact that the "holy ones" are brought into the picture indicates that they are the instrumentalities for bringing torment on the wicked. How could this be? Well, they proclaim the message that points to the eternal destruction awaiting the worshipers of the "wild beast" and its "image." This message puts these false worshipers in torment, giving them no rest day or night. That is why they try everything within their power to silence God's servants. The resulting persecution calls for endurance on the part of the "holy ones." Finally, when the worshipers of the "wild beast" and its "image" are destroyed as by "fire and sulphur," the evidence of that total destruction will, like smoke, ascend for all time to come.

The completeness of that destruction might be illustrated by what befell the cities of Sodom and Gomorrah. The disciple Jude wrote: "Sodom and Gomorrah and the cities about them . . . are placed before us as a warning example by undergoing the judicial punishment of everlasting fire." (Jude 7) The fire that destroyed those cities had stopped burning long before Jude wrote his letter. But the permanent, "everlasting" evidence of that fire's destructiveness remained, for those cities continued nonexistent.

## ETERNAL TORMENT DOES NOT HARMONIZE WITH GOD'S PERSONALITY

That total destruction, not conscious torment for all eternity, is the punishment meted out to those persisting in rebellion also agrees with what God reveals about himself in his Word the Bible. Jehovah God has tender feelings toward his human creation as well as his animal creation.

Consider for a moment God's law about a working bull: "You must not muzzle a bull while it is threshing." (Deuteronomy 25:4) This law reflected God's compassionate concern and care for unreasoning animals. The bull was not to be tormented by being forcibly prevented from satisfying its desire to feed on some of the grain it was threshing.

Far greater is God's concern and love for humankind than for the unreasoning animals. As Jesus Christ reminded his disciples: "Five sparrows sell for two coins of small value, do they not? Yet not one of them goes forgotten before God. But even the hairs of your heads are all numbered. Have no fear; you are worth more than many sparrows."—Luke 12:6, 7.

Would it not be totally inconsistent, then, for anyone to claim that a God with such tender feelings would literally torment some humans for all eternity? Who of us would want to see someone undergoing the most horrible torture for even an hour? Is it not true that only fiendish persons would delight in seeing others suffer? Does not our inward sense of love and justice go into a state of revolt when we hear that a father tortured his child nearly to the point of death for some act of disobedience? Regardless of how bad the child may have been, we find it impossible to have any tender feelings for such a father.

God's compassionate dealing with imperfect mankind, however, does appeal to our moral sense. It warms our hearts and draws us closer to our Creator. Just think of it: Even when people deserve punishment, God has no pleasure in having to administer it. As the prophet Jeremiah exclaimed with reference to God's judgment that befell unfaithful Jerusalem: "Although he has caused grief, he will also certainly show mercy according to the abundance of his loving-kindness. For not out of his own heart has he afflicted or does he grieve the sons of men."—Lamentations 3:32, 33.

If it is not in his heart to afflict or to grieve humans who deserve punishment, how could Jehovah God for all eternity look approvingly upon the anguish of wicked ones? Furthermore, what purpose would it serve? According to the clergy's unscriptural "hell fire" theory, even if those experiencing the torment wanted to change, they could not do so, nor could they improve their situation. God's Word, however, shows unmistakably that total destruction, not torment, is the punishment for all who persist in wickedness.

Appreciating that Jehovah is a loving and just God, we can rest assured that his purpose for those who want to serve him is grand indeed. With eager anticipation, then, let us examine the Scriptures to learn of the loving provisions that he has made to deliver mankind from bondage to disease and death.

## CHAPTER 15

# A Government That Will Conquer Man's Enemy Death

GOD'S original purpose for man was that he might live and enjoy life on a paradise earth. We can have confidence that this purpose will be realized. It is backed by God's dependable promise that man's enemy death will be conquered, destroyed.—1 Corinthians 15:26.

A life-span of but seventy or eighty years is not all there is. If that were the full extent of what even lovers of God could hope for, their situation would differ little from that of those who have no regard for God or his Word. But this is not the case. The Bible says: "God is not unrighteous so as to forget your work and the love you showed for his name."—Hebrews 6:10; 11:6.

What is the reward for those who are serving Jehovah God because of their deep love for him and his righteous ways? There is both a present and a future reward. The apostle Paul wrote: "Godly devotion is beneficial for all things, as it holds promise of the life now and that which is to come." (1 Timothy 4:8) Even now obedience to God's law leads to enjoying a contented, happy life. As to the life "which is to come," Romans 6:23 says: "The gift God gives is everlasting life."

Under present conditions, of course, everlasting life may appear undesirable. But it is eternal life under a righteous administration that God has promised. For that promise to become reality, humans must first be freed from the cause of death. What is that cause? The inspired apostle Paul answers: "The sting producing death is sin."—1 Corinthians 15:56.

Already at the time of pronouncing judgment on the rebellious human pair, Adam and Eve, and upon the instigator of rebellion, Jehovah God pointed to the means by which humans would be freed from sin and death. Not to the unreasoning snake used in the deception, but to Satan himself as the "original serpent" God's words were directed: "I shall put enmity between you and the woman and between your seed and her seed. He will bruise you in the head and you will bruise him in the heel." This judgment, recorded at Genesis 3:15, provided the basis for hope for the future offspring of Adam and Eve. It indicated that man's enemy would be conquered. —Revelation 12:9.

Of course, the mere killing of the "original serpent," Satan the Devil, would not be enough to undo all the injury that he caused by influencing the first humans to rebel against God. But just how the undoing would come about remained a secret until such time as God chose to reveal it. —1 John 3:8.

With the aid of the complete Bible, we today can unravel this sacred secret. The "woman" referred to at Genesis 3:15 could not have been Eve. Eve, by her course of rebellion, aligned herself with the "original serpent," thus making herself a part of his "seed." Then, too, no female descendant of Adam and Eve could be that woman. Why not? Because the 'seed of the woman' had to possess power far greater than that of a mere man in order to crush the "original serpent," the invisible spirit person Satan the Devil. To produce such a mighty "seed," the "woman" would have to be, not human, but spiritual.

At Galatians 4:26 this "woman" is identified as "Jerusalem above." This is very significant. How so?

The ancient city of Jerusalem was the capital of the kingdom of Judah. Because the first Judean king, David, established his seat of government there, Jerusalem from his time onward produced the kings for the nation. Therefore it would only be natural to expect that the "Jerusalem above" would produce a king. This factor pointed to a heavenly government, with a heavenly king, as the agency for putting an end to sin and death.

The "Jerusalem above" is no literal woman or city. It is a symbolic, spiritual city. Being heavenly, it is composed of mighty spirit persons, angels. So, then, for one from among these spirit persons to be designated as king would mean that the "Jerusalem above" had produced an heir to a kingdom. Did such a thing happen?

### THE KING IS BROUGHT FORTH

That is exactly what happened in the year 29 C.E. At that time the man Jesus was anointed by God's holy spirit to become King-Designate. This occurred at the time he presented himself to John the Baptist for immersion in water. As to what took place, the Bible reports: "After being baptized Jesus immediately came up from the water; and, look! the heavens were opened up, and he saw descending like a dove God's spirit coming upon him. Look! Also, there was a voice from the heavens that said: 'This is my Son, the beloved, whom I have approved.' " —Matthew 3:16, 17.

Some months later Jesus began proclaiming: "Repent, you people, for the kingdom of the heavens has drawn near." (Matthew 4:17) Yes, the kingdom had drawn near in the person of the King-Designate.

Though born as a man on earth, Jesus had had a prehuman existence. He himself said: "No man has ascended into heaven but he that descended from heaven, the Son of man." (John 3:13) In calling attention to Jesus' outstanding example of humility, the inspired apostle Paul wrote: "He emptied himself and took a slave's form and came to be in the likeness of men." (Philippians 2:5-7) As to how this transferal from heavenly to earthly life came about, we have the recorded conversation of the angel Gabriel with the virgin Mary:

> "The angel said to her: 'Have no fear, Mary, for you have found favor with God; and, look! you will conceive in your womb and give birth to a son, and you are to call his name Jesus. This one will be great and will be called Son of the Most High; and Jehovah God will give him the throne of David his father, and he will rule as king over the house of Jacob forever, and there will be no end of his kingdom.'
>
> "But Mary said to the angel: 'How is this to be, since I am having no intercourse with a man?' In answer the angel said to her: 'Holy spirit will come upon you, and power of the Most High will overshadow you. For that reason also what is born will be called holy, God's Son.' "—Luke 1:30-35.

Thus, as one of the sons of God making up the "Jerusalem above," Jesus had his life transferred from heaven to the womb of the virgin Mary and was born a perfect human baby. Such a miracle may sound unbelievable to some, yet that casts no valid doubt on the actuality of the event. Surely the One who made it possible for a complete person to develop from an egg cell that is smaller than the period at the end of this sentence could, by means of his spirit or active force, transfer life from the heavens to the earth. And since Jesus' life had been transferred in this way in order for him to become the permanent heir of King David, he actually came forth from the "Jerusalem above."

As foretold in God's prophecy of Genesis 3:15, Jesus experienced a 'heel wound' from the "original serpent" when he was nailed to an executional stake on Nisan 14 of the year 33 C.E. Unlike a crushing in the head from which there is no recovery, that 'heel wound' was but temporary. On the third day God raised Jesus up from the dead, granting him the "power of an indestructible life." (Acts 10:40; Hebrews 7:16) As an immortal spirit person, the King Jesus Christ is in position to crush the "original serpent" in the head and undo all the damage that that one has caused.

## ASSOCIATE RULERS

Jesus Christ is the main one of that composite "seed." By means of him Almighty God will crush Satan the Devil under the feet of Jesus' associates in the heavenly kingdom. (Revelation 20:1-3) Writing to those in line for rulership, the Christian apostle Paul stated: "The God who gives peace will crush Satan under your feet shortly." (Romans 16:20) Who are these associate rulers?

In the last book of the Bible, Revelation, the

number is given as 144,000. Describing what he saw in vision, the writer of Revelation, the apostle John, says: "Look! the Lamb [Jesus Christ, who died a death like a sacrificial lamb] standing upon the Mount Zion, and with him a hundred and forty-four thousand having his name and the name of his Father written on their foreheads. . . . These are the ones that keep following the Lamb no matter where he goes. These were bought from among mankind [not just one nation of people like the Israelites] as firstfruits to God and to the Lamb."—Revelation 14:1-4.

It is indeed appropriate that the 144,000 are depicted as being with the Lamb on Mount Zion. Mount Zion of the ancient city of Jerusalem was the place from which the kings of Judah ruled, the site of the royal palace. It was also at Mount Zion that David pitched a tent for the sacred ark (chest) of the covenant in which were placed the two tablets of stone inscribed with the Ten Commandments. Later that ark was transferred to the innermost compartment of the temple built by David's son Solomon a short distance away on Mount Moriah. The term Zion, in time, came to include Moriah. Thus Zion had prominent association with kingship as well as priesthood. —2 Samuel 6:12, 17; 1 Kings 8:1; Isaiah 8:18.

This agrees with the fact that Jesus is both King and Priest, combining both offices as did Melchizedek of ancient Salem. Therefore Hebrews 6:20 speaks of Jesus as having "become a high priest according to the manner of Melchizedek forever." In the capacity of King-Priest, Jesus rules from heavenly Mount Zion.

His fellow rulers are also priests. As a body they are called a "royal priesthood." (1 Peter

2:9) Of their function, Revelation 5:10 tells us: "You [Christ] made them to be a kingdom and priests to our God, and they are to rule as kings over the earth."

## PURPOSE OF THE ADMINISTRATION

A principal concern of the King-Priest Jesus Christ and his associate priestly rulers is to bring all humankind into unity with Jehovah God. This means the removal of all traces of sin and imperfection, for only those who reflect God's image perfectly can stand on their own merit before him. That the administrative Kingdom is part of God's administration of affairs for bringing this about is indicated at Ephesians 1:9-12:

"[God] made known to us the sacred secret of his will. It is according to his good pleasure which he purposed in himself for an administration at the full limit of the appointed times, namely, to gather all things together again in the Christ, the things in the heavens and the things on the earth. Yes, in him, in union with whom we were also assigned as heirs, in that we were foreordained according to the purpose of him who operates all things according to the way his will counsels, that we should serve for the praise of his glory."

Since Jesus Christ is sinless and in perfect harmony with Jehovah God, the bringing of all things into unity with him results in mankind's being brought into unity with Jehovah God. This is clear from the fact that after this aspect of the Kingdom's work is completed, the Bible says that Jesus Christ "hands over the kingdom to his God and Father."—1 Corinthians 15:24.

To accomplish the tremendous task of perfecting humankind, the heavenly rulers will also be using earthly representatives, men of outstanding devotion to righteousness. (Psalm 45:16; Isaiah 32:1, 2) These men will have to meet the qualifications the King Jesus Christ looks for in those whom he entrusts with responsibility. Two basic qualifications are humility and self-sacrificing love. Said Jesus: "You know that the rulers of the nations lord it over them and the great men wield authority over them. This is not the way among you; but whoever wants to become great among you must be your minister, and whoever wants to be first among you must be your slave." (Matthew 20:25-27) He also said: "This is my commandment, that you love one another just as I have loved you. No one has love greater than this, that someone should surrender his soul in behalf of his friends."—John 15:12, 13.

Would you not feel secure under Kingdom representatives who reflect such love and humility, who would genuinely care for you?

There will be no problems in communication between the heavenly government and the earthly representatives of the King Jesus Christ. In times past Jehovah God transmitted messages to his servants on earth by means of angels and his invisible active force. (Daniel 10:12-14; 2 Peter 1:21) Why, even men have been able to transmit and receive messages to and from capsules and space stations circling far above the earth. If imperfect men can do such things, why should anyone think that this would be too difficult for perfect heavenly rulers?

However, before the Kingdom administration of Jesus Christ and his fellow rulers can proceed with the work of bringing mankind into unity with God, all opposing forces must be removed. There is not the slightest indication that those governing mankind today are willing to hand over their sovereignty to Jesus Christ and his associate rulers. They scoff at the idea that a heavenly government will take full control over earth's affairs. That is why they will have to be forced to recognize the authority of God's kingdom by his Christ. This will be at the cost of their ruling positions as well as their lives. As the Bible tells us: "In the days of those kings the God of heaven will set up a kingdom that will never be brought to ruin. And the kingdom itself will not be passed on to any other people. It will crush and put an end to all these kingdoms, and it itself will stand to times indefinite."—Daniel 2:44.

After clearing out all opposition, the Kingdom administration will set itself to the task of liberating humans from sickness and death. How will this be accomplished?

## CHAPTER 16

# An Earth Free from Sickness and Death

WHAT grand relief an earth forever free from sickness and death would mean for us humans! It would put an end to the bitter tears shed in expression of grief and suffering. Gone would be the excruciating pain and horrible deformities that sickness can bring. No longer would the ravages of old age weaken humans, often bringing them to a state of hopeless despair and helplessness. People everywhere would be enjoying youthful strength and vigor. Not a single mournful sound would ever come forth from their lips!

This is not based on idle imagination. It is what Jehovah God has purposed. He has far more in mind for mankind than just a few years of life filled with problems and suffering.—Revelation 21:3, 4.

## COULD IT LEAD TO TREMENDOUS PROBLEMS?

But would an earth free from sickness and death give rise to other serious problems? Do you wonder: Where would all the people live? Would not the end of sickness and death quickly bring about crowded conditions, making life unpleasant, and leading to great food shortage?

It was never God's purpose to overpopulate the earth. To the perfect Adam and Eve, God said: "Be fruitful and become many and fill the earth." (Genesis 1:28) There is quite a difference between 'filling' the earth and overpopulating it. If someone asked you to fill a glass with juice, you would not keep on pouring until the glass overflowed. Once the glass was sufficiently filled, you would stop pouring. Similarly, once the earth was comfortably filled with humankind, God would see to it that further population growth stopped on this planet.

Moreover, we should not, on the basis of what we see or hear today, misjudge earth's ability to provide a home for us and to sustain human and animal life. While large populations are jammed together in cities, vast regions of the earth are sparsely populated. If the present population were evenly distributed, there would be about six acres of fertile land for every man, woman and child. This would be more than ample room indeed!

The hunger that so many humans must endure in various parts of the earth is not because the full capability of the soil to produce has been reached. Rather, widespread food shortage stems mainly from an unequal distribution of food supplies. Whereas much is produced in certain areas and surpluses exist, in other places there are extreme shortages. Actually, the earth could produce much more than it does at present. Back in 1970 the United Nations Food and Agriculture Organization estimated the world's agricultural potential to be great enough to feed about forty-two times as many people as the present world population.

What man has already done in some regions of the earth gives some indication of what great possibilities there are for increasing earth's productivity.

The Imperial Valley of California was once an inhospitable, uncultivated desert. But irrigation of the mineral-rich desert soil has made this valley one of the richest agricultural regions in the United States.

With about half the farmland, Europe, through more intensive cultivation, produces about as much food as North America.

Truly there can be no question that more land could be brought under more intensive cultivation, and that without spoiling the beauty of forests and meadows.

There is yet another factor that will assure an ample food supply for an earth comfortably filled with animal and human life. What is that? It is the divine help and direction that will then be given to mankind under the administration of God's kingdom by his Son Jesus Christ. No one knows the earth better than does God, for he is its Creator. And under the wise administration of his kingdom the land will yield abundantly. As was the experience of ancient Israel when faithful, so it will be then: "The earth itself will certainly give its produce; God, our God, will bless us."—Psalm 67:6.

Dry deserts and other unproductive areas, occupying millions of acres, will doubtless be reclaimed on a large scale. Receiving divine help in getting needed water is not without historical parallel. Back in the sixth century B.C.E., in fulfillment of God's prophetic promises, thousands of Jewish exiles returned to Jerusalem from Babylon. (Ezra 2:64-70) They evidently took a direct route through the inhospitable Syrian Desert. Yet God provided what they needed to keep alive. Even regarding their homeland he had predicted: "In the wilderness waters will have burst out, and torrents in the desert plain."—Isaiah 35:6.

Since God did this in the past, we have good reason to expect that under the administration of his kingdom by Christ this will be done on a far grander scale.

We need not fear that the ushering in of an earth free from sickness and death will give rise to unpleasant conditions. Not only will there be no overcrowding, but everyone will be able to eat food to satisfaction.

The administration in the hands of God's appointed King, Jesus Christ, and his 144,000 fellow rulers will see to it that earth's inhabitants are well cared for. Pointing to the abundance of wholesome food to be enjoyed, the prophecy of Isaiah states: "Jehovah of armies will certainly make for all the peoples, in this mountain, a banquet . . . of well-oiled dishes filled with marrow, of wine kept on the dregs, filtered."—Isaiah 25:6.

We can have confidence in Jehovah God, the One of whom the Bible declares: "You are opening your hand and satisfying the desire of every living thing." (Psalm 145:16) Never has he failed to fulfill his promises. As the Scriptures say of ancient Israel: "Not a promise failed out of all the good promise that Jehovah had made to the house of Israel; it all came true."—Joshua 21:45.

## HOW SICKNESS AND DEATH WILL PASS AWAY

Besides promising to provide the material things that humans need in order to enjoy life, Jehovah God has promised something worth much more. What is that? Relief from sickness and death. His declared purpose about the grand banquet mentioned in Isaiah is, in fact, followed up by the promise: "He will actually swallow up death forever, and the Sovereign Lord Jehovah will certainly wipe the tears from all faces." —Isaiah 25:8.

In harmony with God's promise here expressed, the Kingdom administration in the hands of Jesus Christ and his associate rulers will be working toward bringing about the liberation of humankind from death. As sickness and death have come about through our being born imperfect sinners due to inheritance from the first man Adam, the death-dealing effects of sin must be counteracted. How?

The basis for doing so must be an arrangement that satisfies justice. Logically it must be an arrangement that offsets the damage caused by the rebellion of Adam. What Adam lost must be regained. The price would have to be a ransom having the exact value of what Adam lost, namely, perfect human life with all its rights and prospects.

None of Adam's sinful descendants could provide such a ransom. This is made clear at Psalm 49:7: "Not one of them can by any means redeem even a brother, nor give to God a ransom for him." But Christ Jesus could do so, for he was a perfect man, and he willingly laid down his life, thereby giving "his soul a ransom in exchange for many."—Matthew 20:28.

On the basis of his sacrificing his own perfect human life, Jesus Christ is in position to apply the benefits of his atoning sacrifice for the uplift of mankind from enslavement to sin. As sinful tendencies have become part of the human make-up, it will take time and help to overcome these. Under the Kingdom in the hands of Jesus Christ, all its human subjects will receive training in the way of righteousness.—Revelation 20:12; Isaiah 26:9.

However, this does not necessarily mean that those suffering from a serious physical disability or deformity are going to have to wait a long period of time during which they will finally recover from their affliction. When Jesus Christ was here on the earth, he healed the sick and afflicted instantly, miraculously. A number of cures he performed from a distance, while he was unseen by the afflicted ones and not in immediate touch with them. (Matthew 8:5-13; 15:21-28; Luke 7:1-10) Therefore any seriously handicapped persons, like a person with one leg or one arm, living when the Kingdom begins administering all of earth's affairs can hope for miraculous, instantaneous healing at God's appointed time. Marvelous indeed it will be to see sight restored to the blind, hearing to the deaf and soundness of body to the disfigured, maimed and deformed!

The bringing of humans to full perfection in body and mind, however, will be a gradual process, requiring the application of Jesus' atoning sacrifice and obedience to the direction of the Kingdom administration. What will take place might be compared to rehabilitating a disabled person under the guidance of a skilled therapist. During the course of his training the disabled person may make many mistakes but eventually he may come to the point where he is able to live a useful life without having to depend on others. The progress he makes depends on his response to the help given.

## QUALIFICATIONS OF THOSE REHABILITATING IMPERFECT HUMANS

In rehabilitating the human race, Jesus Christ has all the needed qualifications. Having lived as a man on earth, he has personal acquaintance with the problems of imperfect humans. Though perfect, he, nevertheless, experienced suffering and sorrow, to the point of shedding tears. The Bible record tells us: "In the days of his flesh Christ offered up supplications and also petitions to the One who was able to save him out of death, with strong outcries and tears, and he was favorably heard for his godly fear. Although he was a Son, he learned obedience from the things he suffered."—Hebrews 5:7, 8.

As a result of what Jesus Christ experienced on earth, we can have confidence that he will be an understanding ruler. He will not deal harshly with his subjects, for he willingly laid down his life for mankind. (1 John 3:16) Then, too, since he is also the High Priest, Jesus will deal compassionately in freeing from sin those who respect his direction. He will not become impatient with them nor make them feel crushed because of their slipping into an act that does not perfectly reflect the personality of God. With reference to Jesus' priestly service, Hebrews 4:15, 16 says: "We have as high priest, not one who cannot sympathize with our weaknesses, but one who has been tested in all respects like ourselves, but without sin. Let us, therefore, approach with freeness of speech to the throne of undeserved kindness, that we may obtain mercy and find undeserved kindness for help at the right time."

While growing to perfection, humans will still be committing sins unintentionally. But by repenting and asking for forgiveness of God through their High Priest Jesus Christ, they will be forgiven and will continue to receive help in overcoming their weaknesses. Depicting the divine provisions for life and healing, Revelation 22:1, 2 speaks of "a river of water of life, clear as crystal, flowing out from the throne of God and of the Lamb down the middle of its broad way. And on this side of the river and on that side there were trees of life producing twelve crops of fruit, yielding their fruits each month. And the leaves of the trees were for the curing of the nations."

Those associated with Jesus Christ in rulership are likewise well qualified to help humankind.

These fellow rulers include both men and women from a great variety of walks of life. (Galatians 3:28) Some of them came from backgrounds that had involved them in such conduct as fornication, adultery, homosexuality, stealing, drunkenness, extortion and the like. But they repented, turned around and began living a clean life, to the praise and honor of God. (1 Corinthians 6:9-11) At the time of their death all who become associate king-priests of Jesus Christ must be found to be lovers and practicers of righteousness, haters of bad, and persons who unselfishly devoted themselves to further the welfare of fellowmen. —Romans 12:9; James 1:27; 1 John 3:15-17; Jude 23.

Maintaining a clean standing before God has not been easy for them. They have been subjected to tremendous pressures to adopt the world's selfish ways. Many have had to face external pressures in the form of reproach, physical abuse and general dislike and scorn. As to what they should expect, Jesus Christ told them: "People will deliver you up to tribulation and will kill you, and you will be objects of hatred by all the nations." (Matthew 24:9) Additionally, all during the course of their life they have had to struggle to combat their own sinful tendencies. One of them, the apostle Paul, said of himself: "I pummel my body and lead it as a slave, that, after I have preached to others, I myself should not become disapproved somehow."—1 Corinthians 9:27.

Truly, then, this body of 144,000 king-priests can sympathize with the problems of the Kingdom's human subjects. They themselves had to contend with them and proved themselves loyal to God despite great difficulties.

## IDEAL CONDITIONS ON EARTH

On earth, too, everything will be just right for assisting humans to grow to perfection. Only those who have shown themselves to be desirous of doing the divine will with a complete heart will remain after the Kingdom destroys its enemies. This means that the human greed and selfishness that have largely been responsible for polluting the food we eat, the water we drink and the air we breathe will be things of the past. The survivors will not be plagued by divisive racial and national barriers. United in the worship of Jehovah God, all will act as brothers and pursue peace. Even the wild animals will do no harm to man or his domestic animals. The prophetic words of Isaiah 11:6-9 will then go beyond a spiritual fulfillment and witness a physical fulfillment:

> "The wolf will actually reside for a while with the male lamb, and with the kid the leopard itself will lie down, and the calf and the maned young lion and the well-fed animal all together; and a mere little boy will be leader over them. And the cow and the bear themselves will feed; together their young ones will lie down. And even the lion will eat straw just like the bull. And the sucking child will certainly play upon the hole of the cobra; and upon the light aperture of a poisonous snake will a weaned child actually put his own hand. They will not do any harm or cause any ruin in all my holy mountain; because the earth will certainly be filled with the knowledge of Jehovah as the waters are covering the very sea."

Through the Kingdom administration Jehovah God will be turning his attention to humans in a special way. This is portrayed in a prophetic vision recorded in the Bible book of Revelation. After comparing the extension of the Kingdom's power to the coming down of New Jerusalem out of heaven, the account tells us: "[God] will wipe out every tear from their eyes, and death will be no more, neither will mourning nor outcry nor pain be anymore. The former things have passed away."—Revelation 21:2-4.

Think of what that means. This present life with its pains and sorrows is definitely not all there is. Humankind will be freed from all mental, emotional and physical pain resulting from imperfection. Mental anguish over uncertainties or grave calamities and dangers will be a thing of the past. The depression, emptiness and loneliness associated with emotional pain will be no more. Never again will people cry out or groan due to severe physical pain. Bitter tears will no longer fill their eyes and stream down their cheeks. There will be no reason for anyone to give way to expressions of grief. Restored to perfection of mind and body, humans will find real pleasure in life for all eternity. Would you not want to be among those to enjoy these blessings from God?

## CHAPTER 17

# What Everlasting Life on Earth Offers Us

LIFE in good health and under pleasant conditions for more than seventy or eighty years is certainly a desirable thing. In fact, scientists have devoted scores of years to research ways to combat aging and disease. They often express the view that an average life-span of a hundred years is a goal to be worked toward.

However, the thought of a never-ending life-span does not seem to have the same appeal. Many persons are inclined to argue: 'Without sickness, death and some troubles we would lose appreciation for good things. Everlasting life on earth would be boring. We would run out of things to do.' Perhaps you have heard people express such thoughts, but is that the way you personally view life? Really, is that kind of reasoning sound?

Do we, for example, need sickness so as not to become bored with good health? People do not lose joy in living because they feel well. Security, pleasant surroundings, interesting and productive work, and wholesome food do not cause people to tire of life. Is it not, rather, a lack of food, unpleasant surroundings, trouble and friction that make life disagreeable? A man does not have to cut off one hand to appreciate the other one, does he? We can enjoy and appreciate good things without experiencing bad.

Life in human perfection does not mean that everyone will be doing all things equally well and with the same intense interest. What the Bible holds forth is the promise of life without sickness and death. (Revelation 21:3, 4) Healthy people today are not all alike, so why should anyone conclude that bodily and mental perfection would make people virtual copies of one another? People will still vary as to personality. They will have varying preferences as to work, building, home decoration, landscaping, food and drink, entertainment, the fine arts and the like. Their personal likes and preferences will have a strong bearing on the skills and fields of activity for which they will show a preference.

But is there really enough for humans to do on earth to keep them active for an eternity? Would not increase in knowledge eventually come to a standstill because we would have done everything?

## MUCH CAN BE DONE

Reflect on your own life now. Do you feel that your capabilities are being used to the full or ever will be? How many things are there that you feel capable of doing and would like to accomplish —if only you had the time and needed assets?

Perhaps you would like to develop some talent, in music, painting, sculpture or carving, or to learn something about woodworking, mechanics, designing or architecture, or to study history, biology, astronomy or mathematics, or to take up the cultivation of certain plants or the breeding of animals, birds or fish. Possibly you would like to travel, to see new lands. Many would like to do, not just one, but a number of these things. But even if you had the needed assets, time would simply not permit you to do all the things you would like to do.

Furthermore, does not limited time also subject you to a certain degree of pressure to get things done? Would it not be a delight to do things without having to feel rushed?

Little danger exists of running out of things to do. Our home, this earth, is filled with such a great variety of plant and creature life that there is limitless potential for learning new things and putting our acquired knowledge to use. Many are the secrets that are just begging to be discovered. Think of it: There are over 30,000 varieties of fish, about 3,000 types of amphibians, about 5,000 sorts of mammals and more than

9,000 kinds of birds. Insects, the most numerous of earth's living creatures, number about 800,000 varieties. Scientists believe that between one and ten million varieties may still remain to be discovered. Added to this are hundreds of thousands of varieties of plants.

How many of us know even the barest fraction of earth's living things by name? Still more limited is our knowledge of their interesting habits and the vital role each plays in the continuance of life on earth. The potential for increased knowledge is stupendous.

You may have never heard of the tropical freshwater fish known as the cichlid. Yet one scientist remarked regarding his study of them: "For me, cichlids have proved an absorbing 14-year study." Think how many years it would take to study thousands of living creatures and plants—and with real benefit.

Take as an example the lowly barnacle. This creature gives man considerable trouble when it attaches itself to ships. Barnacles have to be scraped off the ships, as their presence in great number causes considerable drag and may increase fuel consumption as much as 40 percent. One might be inclined to think that little could be learned from a creature that seemingly makes such a nuisance of itself. But not so.

The cement by means of which the barnacle becomes firmly attached is about 3/10,000 of an inch thick. Yet its resistance to being sheared from the surface exceeds 7,000 pounds per square inch. This is twice the strength of the epoxy glues that have been used in recent years for spacecraft. When subjected by researchers to a temperature of 662 degrees Fahrenheit, barnacle cement did not melt, and it withstood a temperature of 383 degrees Fahrenheit below zero without cracking or peeling. Barnacle cement was also found to be resistant to most solvents. Its outstanding properties have incited researchers to try to produce an artificial barnacle cement, a "Superglue."

Thus, knowledge gained through research can bring benefits to man. Today there is no way of knowing just how many things done by earth's living things could be utilized or duplicated by man for his use. What has been learned is enough to show that the reservoir of knowledge has barely been tapped.

Even in areas where man has done considerable research much remains to be discovered. For example, one of the amazing things done by green plants is changing water and carbon dioxide into sugar. This process, known as photosynthesis, still baffles man despite some two centuries of research. Laurence C. Walker, a plant physiologist, noted that "if the secret unfolded, man could probably feed the world—using a factory the size of a common school building."

All mankind could benefit tremendously by learning more about plant and creature life. By understanding the interdependency of living things and their needs, man could avoid unknowingly upsetting the balance of life. Accurate knowledge would help him to avoid injuring himself and other living things.

For instance, if the harmful effects of DDT had been fully understood and man had acted in harmony with his knowledge, widespread pollution could have been avoided. But, sadly, man made indiscriminate use of DDT. What has been the result? Dr. Lorenzo Tomatis of the International Agency for Research on Cancer in France states: "There is no animal, no water, no soil on this earth which at present is not contaminated with DDT." In some cases DDT contamination has built up in animals and birds to the point of killing them. Truly, accurate knowledge could have prevented this tragic contamination.

Man could also continue to learn about sound, light, chemical reactions, electronics, minerals and a host of other inanimate things. And that still leaves the vast reaches of outer space largely unexplored. What a field for investigation this is! The universe contains billions of galaxies or star systems, and these galaxies may embrace billions of stars.—Psalm 8:3, 4.

Not to be overlooked is the fact that, even without long years of study, animate and inanimate things can stir human creativity and imagination. The colors and designs found among plants, animals and inanimate things not only delight the eye but provide a limitless source of ideas for the decorative arts. There is no reason to fear that human creativity would eventually cease to be stimulated and that life would become drab and uninteresting.

But even if there were a remote possibility of reaching the point of attaining complete knowledge of the earth and all life on it, would that in itself make life boring? Consider: In a year a person may eat more than a thousand meals. At forty years of age a man might have eaten well over forty thousand meals. But does eating become more boring with the passing of each year? Does the man who has eaten forty thousand meals feel more bored than the one who has eaten about half that number?

There can be true enjoyment even in things that are repeated. Who of us is bored by feeling gentle breezes, by the touch of those whom we love, by the sound of babbling brooks, waves crashing against the shore, birds chirping or singing, by seeing gorgeous sunsets, winding rivers, clear lakes, cascading waterfalls, lush meadows, towering mountains or palm-lined beaches, and by catching the scent of sweet-smelling flowers? —Compare Song of Solomon 2:11-13.

## OPPORTUNITIES TO EXPRESS LOVE

Of course, just learning and applying what we learn would not be enough to make everlasting life rich and meaningful. We humans have an inherent need to love and to be loved. When we feel that others need, appreciate and love us, we want life to continue. It warms our hearts to know that others miss us when we are away, that they long to see us again. Association with dear relatives and friends is upbuilding and encouraging. We find happiness in being able to do things for those whom we love, to look out for their welfare.

Everlasting life would set before us endless opportunities to express love and to benefit from the love of others. It would give us the needed time to get to know fellow humans, to come to appreciate their fine qualities and to cultivate intense love for them. Earth's inhabitants are indeed varied—varied in personality, styles of dress, preferences in food, in architecture, in music and other arts. The time it would take to get to know and appreciate billions of humans and to learn from their experience and talents staggers the imagination. But would it not be a pleasure to know the entire human family and to be able to accept each member thereof as a very dear friend?

What everlasting life on earth could offer us is rich and rewarding. How could we possibly be bored when there is so much that we could learn and apply beneficially? How could we possibly tire of expressing love for others to the full? Observed Doctor Ignace Lepp in his book *Death and Its Mysteries:*

"Those who have experienced authentic love and intellectual achievement know well that they can never reach a saturation point. The scientist who consecrates all of his time and energy to research knows that the more he learns, the more there is to learn and the more his appetite for knowledge increases. Likewise, those who love truly know that there is no imaginable limit to the growth of their love."

But when will those opportunities afforded by eternal life become ours? When will God's kingdom by Christ make it possible? And if we should die before that time comes, is there any possibility of our being restored to life?

## CHAPTER 18

# Why Many Now Living Have Opportunity Never to Die

THE time for God's kingdom to begin administering all earth's affairs is at hand. You may be among those to witness the grand blessings it will bring to mankind. That is no unfounded assertion. There is much evidence to back it up, including evidence that you have personally seen.

Many centuries ago Jehovah God revealed the specific time for the conferring of rulership upon the one whom he would designate to be king over the world of mankind. He used symbols to do so and transmitted some of the information by means of a dream.

That such means of communication were used by God to convey this vital information to men should not give rise to doubts. Consider what modern men now do in transmitting information. Cryptic messages are sent in code through space. Thereafter these coded messages are "unscrambled" by either men or machines. This manner of conveying information is purposeful. It conceals the meaning of the information from those not entitled to it.

Similarly, God's use of symbolisms has not been without purpose. The understanding of such symbolisms requires diligent study. But many people are unwilling to take the time to understand, because of having no real love for God and truth. Hence, the "sacred secrets of the

kingdom" remain hidden to them.—Matthew
13:11-15.

## AN ANCIENT PROPHETIC DREAM

One of those "sacred secrets" is contained in
the Bible book of Daniel. That book provides
essentials for determining the time for the giving
of royal authority to God's appointed king. In
the fourth chapter of that book you will find
narrated a divinely sent dream of King Nebuchadnezzar of Babylon. What was the intent or purpose of this dream and its fulfillment? The record
states:

"That people living may know that the Most High
is Ruler in the kingdom of mankind and that to the
one whom he wants to, he gives it and he sets up
over it even the lowliest one of mankind."—Daniel
4:17.

The content of the dream was basically this:
An immense tree was seen being chopped down
at the command of a "holy one," an angel. The
stump of the tree was then banded to prevent it
from sprouting. It was to remain thus banded
amid the "grass of the field" for "seven times."
—Daniel 4:13-16.

What was the meaning of this dream? The
inspired explanation of the prophet Daniel to
Nebuchadnezzar was:

"The tree that you beheld, . . . it is you, O king,
because you have grown great and become strong,
and your grandeur has grown great and reached to
the heavens, and your rulership to the extremity of
the earth.

"And because the king beheld a watcher, even a
holy one, coming down from the heavens, who was
also saying: 'Chop the tree down, and ruin it. However, leave its rootstock itself in the earth, but with
a banding of iron and of copper, among the grass

of the field, and with the dew of the heavens let it become wet, and with the beasts of the field let its portion be until seven times themselves pass over it,' this is the interpretation, O king, and the decree of the Most High is that which must befall my lord the king. And you they will be driving away from men, and with the beasts of the field your dwelling will come to be, and the vegetation is what they will give even to you to eat just like bulls; and with the dew of the heavens you yourself will be getting wet, and seven times themselves will pass over you, until you know that the Most High is Ruler in the kingdom of mankind, and that to the one whom he wants to he gives it.

"And because they said to leave the rootstock of the tree, your kingdom will be sure to you after you know that the heavens are ruling."—Daniel 4:20-26.

So this dream had an initial fulfillment upon King Nebuchadnezzar. For "seven times," or seven literal years, Nebuchadnezzar was insane. His kingdom, however, was held secure for him so that, upon regaining soundness of mind, he again assumed his royal office.—Daniel 4:29-37.

## KINGSHIP OF
## "THE LOWLIEST ONE OF MANKIND"

But this detailed account about the chopped-down tree was not limited in its fulfillment to King Nebuchadnezzar. How do we know this? Because, as stated in the vision itself, it relates to God's kingdom and rulership by the one whom he designates. And who is God's choice for the kingship? The answer given to King Nebuchadnezzar was: "the lowliest one of mankind." —Daniel 4:17.

The facts of history prove undeniably that lowliness has not been displayed by human political rulers. Human governments and their rulers have exalted themselves and they have made a beastly record for themselves, waging sanguinary wars against one another. It should therefore come as no surprise that the Bible compares imperfect human governments or kingdoms to beasts and shows that all of them will eventually be deprived of their rulership. (Daniel 7:2-8) As to who will replace them, the Bible records these words of the prophet Daniel:

"I kept on beholding in the visions of the night, and, see there! with the clouds of the heavens some-one like a son of man happened to be coming; and to the Ancient of Days he gained access, and they brought him up close even before that One. And to him there were given rulership and dignity and king-dom, that the peoples, national groups and languages should all serve even him. His rulership is an indefi-nitely lasting rulership that will not pass away, and his kingdom one that will not be brought to ruin." —Daniel 7:13, 14.

The one here described is none other than Jesus Christ, who is designated in the Scriptures as both the "Son of man" and as the "King of kings and Lord of lords." (Matthew 25:31; Revelation 19:16) He willingly gave up his superior position in the heavens and became a man, a "little lower than angels." (Hebrews 2:9; Philippians 2:6-8) As a man, Jesus Christ, even under extreme provocation, proved himself to be "mild-tempered and lowly in heart." (Matthew 11:29) "When he was being reviled, he did not go reviling in return. When he was suffering, he did not go threatening, but kept on committing himself to the one who judges righteously."—1 Peter 2:23.

The world of mankind viewed Jesus Christ as being of no account, refusing to accord him the honor he rightfully deserved. The situation was as had been foretold by the prophet Isaiah: "He was despised and was avoided by men, a man meant for pains and for having acquaintance with sickness. And there was as if the concealing of one's face from us. He was despised, and we held him as of no account."—Isaiah 53:3.

There can be no question that Jesus fits the description of "the lowliest one of mankind." Hence, the prophetic dream about the chopped-down tree must point to the time when he would receive rulership over the world of mankind. This would be at the end of "seven times." How long are these "times"? When do they start? When do they end?

### THE LENGTH OF THE "SEVEN TIMES"

More than six centuries after Nebuchadnezzar's dream, Jesus Christ appeared on the scene, declaring that "the kingdom of the heavens has drawn near." (Matthew 4:17) He could say this because he, as King-Designate, was present. But he did not at that time receive kingship over the world of mankind. Thus, on one occasion when others wrongly concluded that "the kingdom of God was going to display itself instantly," Jesus Christ gave an illustration showing that a long period of time would be involved before his gaining such kingly power. (Luke 19:11-27) It is, therefore, clear that in the larger fulfillment of Daniel's prophecy the "seven times" cover a period, not of just seven years, but of many centuries.

The evidence is that these "seven times" amounted to 2,520 days, that is, seven prophetic years of 360 days each. This is confirmed in other parts of the Bible that mention "times," "months" and "days." For example, Revelation 11:2 speaks of a period of "forty-two months," or three and a half years. In the next verse the same period is mentioned as being "a thousand two hundred and sixty days." Now, if you were to divide 1,260 days by 42 months, you would get 30 days for each month. A year of 12 months would therefore be 360 days long. On this basis, "seven times," or seven years, would be 2,520 days long (7 x 360).

The correctness of this computation is verified by Revelation 12:6, 14, where 1,260 days are spoken of as "a time and times and half a time," or 'three and a half times' ("three years and a half," *The New English Bible*). Seven being the double of three and a half, "seven times" would equal 2,520 days (2 x 1,260).

Of course, as they relate to Jesus' receiving the kingship over the world of mankind, the "seven times" of Daniel's prophecy span a period of far more than 2,520 twenty-four-hour days. Is there any way to ascertain the length of each of these "days"? Yes, the Bible's formula for prophetic days is: "A day for a year." (Numbers 14:34; Ezekiel 4:6) Applying this to the "seven times," we see that they amount to 2,520 years.

### THE START OF THE "SEVEN TIMES"

Knowing the length of the "seven times," we are now in position to investigate when they began. Again we direct our attention to what happened to Nebuchadnezzar in fulfillment of the prophetic dream about the chopped-down tree. Consider his situation:

At the time that Nebuchadnezzar lost his sanity he was exercising world domination, for Babylon was then the number one power on earth. In Nebuchadnezzar's case the cutting down of the symbolic tree meant a temporary break in his rule as a world sovereign.

The whole intent of what God did in Nebuchadnezzar's case involved rule by the king of God's own choice. Nebuchadnezzar's losing his throne for "seven times" must therefore have been symbolic. Of what? Of a temporary break in rulership or sovereignty by God's arrangement, since, in Nebuchadnezzar's case, Jehovah God was the one who had permitted him to attain the position of world ruler and thereafter took that position away from him temporarily, as the king himself acknowledged. (Daniel 4:34-37) So what befell Nebuchadnezzar must have been symbolic of the removal of sovereignty from a kingdom of God. Hence, the tree itself represented world domination as regards the earth.

At one time the government that had its seat in Jerusalem was a kingdom of God. The rulers of the royal line of David were said to sit upon "Jehovah's throne" and were under command to reign according to his law. (1 Chronicles 29:23) Jerusalem was therefore the seat of God's government in a representative sense.

So when the Babylonians under Nebuchadnezzar destroyed Jerusalem, and the land of its dominion was completely desolated, world rulership passed into Gentile hands without any interference from a kingdom representing Jehovah's sovereignty. The Supreme Sovereign restrained himself from exercising his rulership in this way. This restraining of himself from wielding sovereignty over the earth by a kingdom of his is likened to the banding of the remaining tree stump. At the time of its destruction and total desolation Jerusalem, as the capital city representing the governmental expression of Jehovah's sovereignty, began to be "trampled on." That means, therefore, that the "seven times" had their start at the time that Nebuchadnezzar destroyed Jerusalem and the land of Judah was completely desolated. When did that event occur?

The Bible and secular history can be used to establish 607 B.C.E. as the date for this event.* The evidence is as follows:

Secular historians are in agreement that Babylon fell to Cyrus the Persian in the year 539 B.C.E. This date is substantiated by all available historical records of ancient times. The Bible reveals that in his first year of rule, Cyrus issued a decree permitting the exiled Israelites to return to Jerusalem and rebuild the temple. There being first the brief rule of Darius the Mede over Babylon, Cyrus' first year of rule toward Babylon evidently extended from 538 to 537 B.C.E. (Daniel 5:30, 31) As considerable distance in traveling was involved, it must have been by the "seventh month" of 537 B.C.E. (rather than 538 B.C.E.) that the Israelites were back in their cities, ending the desolation of Jerusalem and the land of Judah. (Ezra 3:1, 6) Nevertheless, they remained under Gentile domination, and therefore spoke of themselves as 'slaves upon their own land.'—Nehemiah 9:36, 37.

The Bible book of Second Chronicles (36:19-21) shows that a period of seventy years passed from

---

* Modern secular historians do not generally present 607 B.C.E. as the date for this event, but they are dependent on the writings of men who lived centuries after it happened. On the other hand, the Bible contains testimony from eyewitnesses, and it sets out factors that are ignored by secular writers. Furthermore, the fulfillment of Bible prophecy at the end of the "seven times" establishes the date beyond doubt. As to why the Bible's chronological data is more reliable than secular history, see the book *Aid to Bible Understanding*, pp. 322-348.

the time of the destruction of Jerusalem and the desolation of its domain until the restoration. It says:

"He [Nebuchadnezzar] proceeded to burn the house of the true God and pull down the wall of Jerusalem; and all its dwelling towers they burned with fire and also all its desirable articles, so as to cause ruin. Furthermore, he carried off those remaining from the sword captive to Babylon, and they came to be servants to him and his sons until the royalty of Persia began to reign; to fulfill Jehovah's word by the mouth of Jeremiah, until the land had paid off its sabbaths. All the days of lying desolated it kept sabbath, to fulfill seventy years."

Counting back seventy years from the time the Israelites arrived back in their cities, that is, in 537 B.C.E., brings us to 607 B.C.E. It was in that year, therefore, that Jerusalem, the seat of God's government in a representative sense, began to be trampled on by Gentile nations.

## THE END OF THE "SEVEN TIMES"

Jesus Christ referred to this trampling on Jerusalem when he said to his disciples: "Jerusalem will be trampled on by the nations, until the appointed times of the nations are fulfilled." (Luke 21:24) Those "appointed times" were to end 2,520 years after 607 B.C.E. This would be in the year 1914 C.E. Did the trampling on Jerusalem cease then?

True, the earthly city of Jerusalem did not witness the restoration of a king in the royal line of David in 1914 C.E. But such a thing was not to be expected. Why not? The earthly city of Jerusalem no longer had any holy significance from God's viewpoint. While on earth, Jesus Christ stated: "Jerusalem, Jerusalem, the killer of the prophets and stoner of those sent forth to her—how often I wanted to gather your children together in the manner that a hen gathers her brood of chicks under her wings, but you people did not want it! Look! Your house is abandoned to you." (Luke 13:34, 35) Moreover, the kingdom in the hands of Jesus Christ is not an earthly government with Jerusalem or any other city as its capital. It is a heavenly kingdom.

Hence, it was in the invisible heavens that the year 1914 C.E. witnessed the fulfillment of Revelation 11:15: "The kingdom of the world did become the kingdom of our Lord and of his Christ, and he will rule as king forever and ever." What Jerusalem *represented,* that is, the Messianic government ruling with divine approval, was then no longer being trampled on. Once again there was a king of the Davidic dynasty who, by divine appointment, exercised rulership over the affairs of mankind. The visible events that have taken place here on earth in fulfillment of Bible prophecy since 1914 C.E. prove that this is the case.

One of these prophecies is found in the sixth chapter of the Bible book of Revelation. There the giving of royal authority to Jesus Christ and the events following it are described in symbolic terms.

Of Jesus' receiving the kingship the account says: "Look! a white horse; and the one seated upon it had a bow; and a crown was given him, and he went forth conquering and to complete his conquest." (Revelation 6:2) Later on, the book of Revelation unmistakably identifies the rider on that horse, saying: "Look! a white horse. And the one seated upon it is called Faithful and True, and he judges and carries on war in righteousness. . . . And upon his outer garment, even upon his thigh, he has a name written, King of kings and Lord of lords."—Revelation 19:11-16.

As to what would happen here on earth after Jesus' receiving the "crown" of active kingship over the world of mankind, Revelation chapter 6 continues:

"Another came forth, a fiery-colored horse; and to the one seated upon it there was granted to take peace away from the earth so that they should slaughter one another; and a great sword was given him. And when he opened the third seal, I heard the third living creature say: 'Come!' And I saw, and, look! a black horse; and the one seated upon it had a pair of scales in his hand. . . . And when he opened the fourth seal, I heard the voice of the fourth living creature say: 'Come!' And I saw, and, look! a pale horse; and the one seated upon it had the name Death. And Hades was closely following him. And authority was given them over the fourth part of the earth, to kill with a long sword and with food shortage and with deadly plague and by the wild beasts of the earth."—Vss. 4-8.

Have not these words been fulfilled? Did not the sword of global warfare rage from 1914 onward? Indeed! World War I witnessed the slaughter of humans on a scale never known before. Over nine million combatants died from wounds, disease and other causes. Civilian deaths directly or indirectly resulting from the war also ran into the millions. The second world war snuffed out an even greater number of lives. It claimed an estimated fifty-five million civilians and combatants.

Did not food shortage, like a black horse, stalk through the earth? Yes, in many parts of Europe there was famine during and after the World War I period. In Russia millions died. After the second world war came what *The World Book Encyclopedia* (1973) describes as "the greatest world-wide shortage of food in history." And today the grim fact is that one out of every three people on earth is slowly starving or suffering from malnutrition.

Deadly plague also took its toll. In a matter of months, during 1918-1919, the Spanish influenza epidemic alone killed about 20,000,000. No single disaster had ever before caused such a mammoth destruction of life among mankind.

Truly these things have been too big to escape notice. Says Joseph Carter, in his book *1918 Year of Crisis, Year of Change:* "In that autumn [of 1918], horror was piled on horror, for three of the Four Horsemen of the Apocalypse—war, famine, and pestilence—were indeed abroad." To this day the symbolic horsemen have not stopped their ride.

Thus there exists visible evidence that in 1914

C.E. the restraining bands were removed from the symbolic tree stump of Nebuchadnezzar's dream. Jehovah God began exercising authority through the kingdom of his Son, the Lord Jesus Christ. But why did this not improve conditions on earth? Why has the time of Christ's being given ruling authority over mankind been associated with trouble?

This is because Satan the Devil is against God's kingdom by Christ. He fought against it at the time of its being given authority over mankind. But he lost the battle and was ousted along with his demons from the holy heavens. Enraged, he and his demons are stirring up all the trouble they can among mankind to bring everyone and everything to ruin. That is why, after describing the war in heaven and its outcome, the Bible account continues: "Be glad, you heavens and you who reside in them! Woe for the earth and for the sea, because the Devil has come down to you, having great anger, knowing he has a short period of time."—Revelation 12:7-12.

How short is that period of time remaining to the Kingdom's adversary? Jesus Christ revealed that the time of his coming in Kingdom glory and the removal of the ungodly system of things would fall within the lifetime of one generation of people. He said: "Truly I say to you that this generation will by no means pass away until all these things occur."—Matthew 24:3-42.

Hence, some of the generation alive in 1914 C.E. must be among the people to witness Jesus' completing his conquest and taking full control of earth's affairs. That also means that many now living the opportunity never to die. How so?

## WHY MANY NOW LIVING WILL NOT
## EXPERIENCE DEATH

In completing his conquest, Jesus Christ as king will take action only against those who refuse to submit to his rulership. When comforting fellow believers who were suffering persecution, the inspired apostle Paul wrote of this, saying: "It is righteous on God's part to repay tribulation to those who make tribulation for you, but, to you who suffer tribulation, relief along with us at the revelation of the Lord Jesus from heaven with his powerful angels in a flaming fire, as he brings vengeance upon those who do not know God and those who do not obey the good news about our Lord Jesus. These very ones will undergo the judicial punishment of everlasting destruction from before the Lord and from the glory of his strength."—2 Thessalonians 1:6-9.

Certainly not all persons refuse to "know" or recognize God's authority in their lives. Not all are disobedient to the 'good news about Jesus Christ.' Though few, when compared with the world's population, there is a body of Christians who are striving hard to prove themselves to be devoted servants of God and loyal disciples of Jesus Christ. Those whom the day of divine execution finds exclusively devoted to Jehovah God can rest assured that they will not be swept away by that judgment. The Bible says:

"These are the ones that come out of the great tribulation, and they have washed their robes and made them white in the blood of the Lamb. That is why they are before the throne of God; and they are rendering him sacred service day and night in his temple; and the One seated on the throne will spread his tent over them. They will hunger no more nor thirst anymore, neither will the sun beat down upon them nor any scorching heat, because the Lamb, who is in the midst of the throne, will shepherd them, and will guide them to fountains of waters of life. And God will wipe out every tear from their eyes." —Revelation 7:14-17.

The prospect before the great crowd of "tribulation" survivors is, not death, but life. The "Lamb," that is, the Lord Jesus Christ, will be guiding them to "fountains of waters of life." This is not life for merely seventy or eighty years, but forever. He will be applying to them the benefits of his sin-atoning sacrifice, liberating them from sin and its death-dealing effects. As they obediently respond to his help, they will attain to human perfection, with no need to die.

There will be no interference from Satan and his demonic horde to hinder their progress. After the "great tribulation" has brought an end to the earthly wicked system of things, Satan will be abyssed for a thousand years. The Bible's symbolic description of this event reads: "I saw an angel coming down out of heaven with the key of the abyss and a great chain in his hand. And he seized the dragon, the original serpent, who is the Devil and Satan, and bound him for a thousand years. And he hurled him into the abyss and shut it and sealed it over him, that he might not mislead the nations." (Revelation 20:1-3) Thus, as if dead, Satan and his demons will be in no position to cause trouble for humankind.

The Bible clearly pinpoints the generation alive in 1914 C.E. as the one that will yet witness the ushering in of Kingdom rule free from Satanic interference. Hence, many living today will have the opportunity never to die. They will survive the destruction of the present ungodly system and thereafter gradually be freed from sin and brought to human perfection. As sinless humans they will then be exempt from sin's wages—death. —Romans 6:23.

This makes it urgent for you to place yourself on the side of the King Jesus Christ, if you have not already done so, and to live now as one of his loyal subjects. That is what Jehovah's Christian witnesses are endeavoring to do, and they are eager to assist others to do the same.

## CHAPTER 19

# Billions Now Dead Will Soon Live Again

THE Kingdom administration in the hands of Jesus Christ and his 144,000 associate rulers will indeed bestow grand blessings upon the survivors of the "great tribulation." At that time the damaging effects of Adam's plunging himself and his unborn offspring into sin will not be recalled in such a way as to be mentally and emotionally painful. The inspired words of the prophet Isaiah promise: "The former things will not be called to mind, neither will they come up into the heart."—Isaiah 65:17.

For that to be the case, the pain and sorrow resulting from the death-dealing effects of sin must be completely undone. This would include raising to life billions of people now dead. Why?

Well, if you were to survive the "great tribulation," would you be truly happy knowing that dear friends and relatives who had died in years past were still deprived of life and its blessings? Would this not bring pain of heart and mind to you? To remove any possibility of such pain, the dead must be raised. Only if they can be restored to life and be assisted to attain perfection in body and mind will the damaging effects of sin be fully erased.

The Holy Scriptures assure us that the dead in general will live again. They will be given the opportunity to have more than the short life-span that ended at their death. Jehovah God has empowered his Son Jesus Christ to resurrect them. (John 5:26-28) Jesus' being empowered to raise the dead agrees with the fact that he is prophetically referred to in the Bible as the "Eternal Father." (Isaiah 9:6) By raising to life those sleeping in death, Jesus becomes their Father.—Compare Psalm 45:16.

## BASIS FOR BELIEF

For one who accepts the existence of God, there should be no problem in having a firm belief in the resurrection. Is it not reasonable that the One who originally started off human life is also wise enough to restore life to the dead, to re-create dead humans? Jehovah God has personally promised that the dead will live again. He has also performed powerful works that strengthen one's confidence in this promise.

Jehovah God empowered some of his faithful servants actually to raise the dead. At Zarephath, not far from the eastern shore of the Mediterranean Sea, Elijah the prophet resurrected the only son of a widow. (1 Kings 17:21-23) His successor Elisha raised the only son of a prominent, hospitable woman at Shunem, in the northern part of Israel. (2 Kings 4:8, 32-37) Jesus Christ resurrected the daughter of Jairus, a presiding officer of a synagogue near the Sea of Galilee; the only son of a widow at Nain, to the southwest of the Sea of Galilee; and his dear friend Lazarus, who had been dead four days and was buried not far from Jerusalem. (Mark 5:22, 35, 41-43; Luke 7:11-17; John 11:38-45) At Joppa, on the Mediterranean coast, the apostle Peter raised Dorcas (Tabitha) from the dead. (Acts 9:36-42) And the apostle Paul, on a stopover in the Roman province of Asia, resurrected Eutychus after he had tumbled to his death from a third-story window.—Acts 20:7-12.

The most remarkable resurrection was that of Jesus Christ himself. This well-attested historical event provides the strongest proof for there being a resurrection. That is what the apostle Paul pointed out to those assembled at the Areopagus in Athens, Greece: "[God] purposes to judge the inhabited earth in righteousness by a man whom he has appointed, and he has furnished a guarantee to all men in that he has resurrected him from the dead."—Acts 17:31.

Jesus' resurrection was a fact established beyond a shadow of doubt. There were far more than two or three witnesses who could testify to it. Why, on one occasion the resurrected Jesus Christ appeared to upward of five hundred disciples. So well confirmed was his resurrection that the apostle Paul could say that denial of the resurrection meant denial of Christian faith as a whole. He wrote: "If, indeed, there is no resurrection of the dead, neither has Christ been raised up. But if Christ has not been raised up, our preaching is certainly in vain, and our faith is in vain.

Moreover, we are also found false witnesses of God, because we have borne witness against God that he raised up the Christ, but whom he did not raise up if the dead are really not to be raised up."—1 Corinthians 15:13-15.

Early Christians, like the apostle Paul, knew for a certainty that Jesus had been raised from the dead. So powerful was their conviction of being rewarded in the resurrection that they were willing to face severe persecution, even death itself.

## RESURRECTION TO SPIRIT LIFE

The resurrection of Jesus Christ shows that raising the dead does not mean bringing back to life the identical body. Jesus was raised, not to human life, but to spirit life. With reference to this, the apostle Peter wrote: "Why, even Christ died once for all time concerning sins, a righteous person for unrighteous ones, that he might lead you to God, he being put to death in the flesh, but being made alive in the spirit." (1 Peter 3:18) At his resurrection Jesus received a body, not of flesh and blood, but one suitable for heavenly life.—1 Corinthians 15:40, 50.

That spirit body was, of course, invisible to human eyes. Hence, for his disciples to see him after his resurrection, Jesus had to take on flesh. It should be noted that Jesus was not buried with clothing but was wrapped up in fine linen bandages. After his resurrection the bandages remained in the tomb. So, just as Jesus had to materialize clothing, he also took on flesh to make himself visible to his disciples. (Luke 23: 53; John 19:40; 20:6, 7) Strange? No, this was exactly what angels had done prior to this time when they appeared to humans. The fact that Jesus materialized a body of flesh explains why his disciples did not always recognize him at first and why he could appear and disappear suddenly.—Luke 24:15-31; John 20:13-16, 20.

Only the 144,000 joint heirs who are associated with Jesus Christ in rulership will experience a resurrection like his. Discussing that resurrection to spirit life, the Bible tells us:

> "What you sow is not made alive unless first it dies; and as for what you sow, you sow, not the body that will develop, but a bare grain, it may be, of wheat or any one of the rest; but God gives it a body just as it has pleased him, and to each of the seeds its own body. . . .
> "So also is the resurrection of the dead. It is sown in corruption, it is raised up in incorruption. It is sown in dishonor, it is raised up in glory. It is sown in weakness, it is raised up in power. It is sown a physical body, it is raised up a spiritual body. If there is a physical body, there is also a spiritual one. It is even so written: 'The first man Adam became a living soul.' The last Adam became a life-giving spirit. Nevertheless, the first is, not that which is spiritual, but that which is physical, afterward that which is spiritual. The first man is out of the earth and made of dust; the second man is out of heaven. As the one made of dust is, so those made of dust are also; and as the heavenly one is, so those who are heavenly are also. And just as we have borne the image of the one made of dust, we shall bear also the image of the heavenly one."
> —1 Corinthians 15:36-49.

### RESURRECTION TO LIFE ON EARTH

But what of those who, unlike Jesus Christ and his 144,000 fellow rulers, will be resurrected to earthly life? Since they have 'returned to the dust,' will God have to reassemble all the atoms that once formed their bodies so that their bodies are identical in every respect to what they were at the moment of death?

No, that simply could not be. Why not? First of all, because this would mean that they would be brought back to life in a condition on the verge of death. Persons resurrected in the past were not brought back in the identical sickly condition that preceded their death. Though not perfect at the time of their resurrection, they had a whole, reasonably sound body.

Moreover, it would not be reasonable to insist that precisely the same atoms be regathered to form their restored body. After death, and through the process of decay, the human body is converted into other organic chemicals. These may be absorbed by plants, and people may eat these plants or their fruit. Thus the atomic elements making up the deceased person can eventually come to be in other people. Obviously, at the time of the resurrection the identical atoms cannot be reassembled in every person brought back from the dead.

What, then, does resurrection mean for the individual? It means his being brought back to life as the same *person*. And what makes an individual the person he is? Is it the chemical substance making up his body? No, inasmuch as the molecules in the body are regularly being replaced. What really distinguishes him from other people, then, is his general physical appearance, his voice, his personality, his experiences, mental growth and memory. So when Jehovah God, by means of his Son Jesus Christ, raises a person from the dead, he evidently will provide that person with a body having the same traits as previously. The resurrected person will have the same memory that he had acquired during his lifetime and he will have the full awareness of that memory. The person will be able to identify himself, and those who knew him will also be able to do so.

'But if a person is thus re-created,' someone may say, 'is he really the same person? Is he not just a copy?' No, for this reasoning overlooks the fact earlier mentioned that even in life our bodies are constantly undergoing change. About seven years ago the molecules making up our bodies were different from the molecules forming them today. We even differ in appearance as the years go by. Yet, do we not have the same fingerprints? Are we not the same persons? Most certainly.

Those to whom the resurrection seems almost unbelievable should reflect on a similarly marvelous process that takes place at the time of

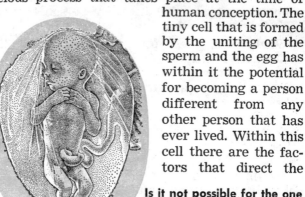

human conception. The tiny cell that is formed by the uniting of the sperm and the egg has within it the potential for becoming a person different from any other person that has ever lived. Within this cell there are the factors that direct the

**Is it not possible for the one who makes a baby grow in its mother's womb also to resurrect the dead?**

building of the individual and the forming of the basic personality he inherits from his parents. Then, of course, his life experiences thereafter add to that personality. Similar to what happens at the time of conception, at the time of the resurrection or re-creation the deceased person will have his personality and life record restored to him, every cell of his body being impressed with the characteristics that make him different from all other persons. And his heart, mind and body will have impressed within them the added qualities, traits and abilities that he developed during his former lifetime.

Regarding the Creator, the inspired psalmist noted: "Your eyes saw even the embryo of me, and in your book all its parts were down in writing, as regards the days when they were formed and there was not yet one among them." (Psalm 139:16) Accordingly, as soon as the genetic combinations are formed at the time of conception, Jehovah God is capable of perceiving and having a record of a child's basic traits. So it is wholly logical that he is capable of having an accurate record by which to re-create one who has died.

We can have confidence in Jehovah's perfect memory. Why, even imperfect humans, by means of videotape, can preserve and construct visible and audible reproductions of persons. Far greater is God's ability to keep such records, for he calls all the numberless stars by name!—Psalm 147:4.

It can be seen, therefore, that resurrection or re-creation is possible because the deceased individual lives in God's memory. Because of his perfect memory of life patterns and his purpose to resurrect the dead, Jehovah God could count deceased men of faith like Abraham, Isaac and Jacob as being alive. That is what Jesus Christ called to the attention of unbelieving Sadducees, saying: "That the dead are raised up even Moses disclosed, in the account about the thornbush, when he calls Jehovah 'the God of Abraham and God of Isaac and God of Jacob.' He is a God, not of the dead, but of the living, for they are all living to him."—Luke 20:37, 38.

There is indeed ample basis for believing in the resurrection or re-creation. True, some may reject the idea. But would you be better off to close your eyes and mind to the evidence and refuse to believe in the resurrection? Would it make it easier for you to lose a dear relative or friend in death? Would you be better prepared to face the grim prospect of your own death?

Knowing that this life is not all there is frees one from the fear of having it cut off prematurely by violent means. This fear has been exploited by Satan the Devil in holding people in slavery, maneuvering them through his earthly agents to do his bidding. (Matthew 10:28; Hebrews 2:14) Afraid of the possibility of being executed, many have failed to follow the dictates of their conscience and have committed dastardly crimes against humanity, as was done in the concentration camps of Nazi Germany.

The person with strong faith in the resurrection, however, is strengthened in his determination to do what is right even if that might mean death for him. To him the life that he will enjoy upon being raised from the dead is far more precious than a few years of life now. He does not want to jeopardize his opportunity to gain everlasting life for what, by comparison, could hardly be called a lengthening of his life. He is like the men of ancient times of whom the Bible book of Hebrews reports: "[They] were tortured because they would not accept release by some ransom [some compromise of what is right], in order that they might attain a better resurrection."—Hebrews 11:35.

Certainly those who have confidence in God's promise to raise the dead are far better off than those who do not have the resurrection hope. They can look to the future without fear.

Biblical evidence shows that this system will soon come to its end, within this generation, and be replaced by a righteous administration in the hands of Jesus Christ and his associate rulers. That is why billions now dead will soon live again and begin to benefit from Kingdom rule. How grand it will be for the "tribulation" survivors to welcome back the dead! Think of the joy of once again being able to have the encouraging companionship of dear friends and beloved relatives, to hear their familiar voices and to see them in good health.

What effect should this have on you? Should it not prompt you to thank God for the marvelous resurrection hope? Should not your gratitude move you to do all that you can to learn about him and then to serve him faithfully?

## CHAPTER 20

# For Whom Will Resurrection
## Bring Benefits?

MANY questions come up about the resurrection of the dead. Who will be resurrected? Infants? Children? Both the righteous and the wicked? Will those who were married be reunited with their former mates?

The Bible does not go into every detail about the resurrection. However, it contains the marvelous promise that the dead will be raised to life and it gives enough particulars to establish faith in that promise. Should its silence about certain matters keep us from appreciating the soundness of that promise?

In our dealings with fellowmen we do not expect every detail to be spelled out, do we? For example, if you were invited to a banquet, you would not ask the one extending the invitation: 'Where will all the people sit? Are you prepared to cook for so many people? How can I be sure you will have enough serving utensils and dishes?' To ask such questions would be an insult, would it not? No one would think of saying to a host: 'First convince me that I will enjoy myself.' Having the invitation and knowing its source should be sufficient for one to be confident that things will go well.

Really, no one would appreciate being called upon to explain or prove each statement that he makes. Let us say that an acquaintance described an experience in saving a person from drowning. If he was a respected friend, we would not ask him to prove that he actually did the things he described. To require this would show lack of confidence and trust. It would be no basis for building and maintaining a friendship. Obviously, then, one who would not accept God's promise of a resurrection without first having every detail clarified could never be counted as His friend. God accepts as his friends only those who exercise faith, who trust his word. (Hebrews 11:6) He provides abundant evidence on which to base such faith, but he does not force people to believe by providing and proving every single detail so that faith is unnecessary.

Thus the absence of certain details serves to test people as to what they are at heart. There are those who have a high opinion of themselves and their own pet ideas, and who follow a course of independence. They do not want to be accountable to anyone. Belief in the resurrection would require them to acknowledge a need to live in harmony with God's will. But this they do not want to do. Hence, due to the absence of certain details about the resurrection, they may find what they consider to be justification for their disbelief. They are much like the Sadducees in the time of Jesus' earthly ministry. The Sadducees refused to believe in the resurrection and pointed to what they thought to be an insurmountable problem. They said to Jesus:

"Teacher, Moses wrote us, 'If a man's brother dies having a wife, but this one remained childless, his brother should take the wife and raise up offspring from her for his brother.' Accordingly there were seven brothers; and the first took a wife and died childless. So the second, and the third took her. Likewise even the seven: they did not leave children behind, but died off. Lastly, the woman also died. Consequently, in the resurrection, of which one of them does she become the wife? For the seven got her as wife."—Luke 20:28-33.

In answering their question, Jesus Christ exposed the wrongness of the Sadducees' reasoning and emphasized the surety of the resurrection promise. He replied:

"The children of this system of things marry and are given in marriage, but those who have been counted worthy of gaining that system of things and the resurrection from the dead neither marry nor are given in marriage. . . . But that the dead are raised up even Moses disclosed, in the account about the thornbush, when he calls Jehovah 'the God of Abraham and God of Isaac and God of Jacob.' He is a God, not of the dead, but of the living, for they are all living to him."—Luke 20:34-38.

## WHY RESURRECTION HOLDS FORTH
## NO PROMISE OF MARRIAGE

On the basis of Jesus' answer to the Sadducees, some may be disturbed about his saying that there will be no marrying among those raised from the dead. They may even think that without marriage the resurrection is something undesirable, that it would not benefit them.

However, when reasoning on Jesus' reply, we do well to remember that we are imperfect. Our likes and dislikes are largely conditioned by the things to which we have become accustomed. So no one really has any basis for being sure that he would not like the future provisions that God will make for the resurrected ones. Then, too, not all the details have been provided. This has really been a kindness on God's part. Why, as imperfect humans, we might at first react unfavorably to things that would actually fill our life with joy in a perfect state. Such details therefore might be beyond our present ability to receive. Christ Jesus showed awareness and consideration of the limitations of imperfect humans, as evident from what he said to his disciples on one occasion: "I have many things yet to say to you, but you are not able to bear them at present."—John 16:12.

Those who will attain a resurrection to immortal spirit life in the heavens have no concept of what it will be like. They cannot compare it with anything they know on earth. Their bodies will be completely different. All sex distinctions belonging to humans will be things of the past for them. So there can be no marrying among those raised to spirit life in the heavens because they all together as a body become the "bride" of Christ.

But what about those who are brought back from the dead to live on earth? Will they be reunited with former marriage mates? No statement in the Bible indicates that this will be the case. The Scriptures definitely show that death dissolves the marriage. Romans 7:2, 3 reads: "A married woman is bound by law to her husband while he is alive; but if her husband dies, she is discharged from the law of her husband . . . so that she is not an adulteress if she becomes another man's."

Hence, if a person chooses to remarry now, he does not have to worry about the effect this might have on a resurrected mate in the future. If singleness is not for him, he does not have to struggle to maintain it in the hope of being reunited in marriage with his former mate in the resurrection. Surely, then, it was a kindness on God's part not to require former marriage relationships to be in force at the time of a person's resurrection, as the Sadducees erroneously thought.

While we do not know where on earth or with whom the resurrected ones will live, we can rest assured that whatever arrangement exists will contribute to the happiness of the resurrected ones. God's gifts, including the resurrection, will wholly satisfy the desires and needs of obedient mankind. His gifts are perfect, flawless. (James 1:17) The generous gifts that we have already received as expressions of his love convince us of that.

## CHILDREN AND OTHERS TO BE RAISED

What of children who die? Will they too return to life when righteousness prevails on this earth? Surely that is what loving parents would want for any children that they may have lost in death. And there is solid basis for entertaining such a hope.

Among those reported in the Bible as having been resurrected were children. The daughter of Jairus, who lived in Galilee, was about twelve years of age; Jesus brought her back to life. (Luke 8:42, 54, 55) The boys who were raised from the dead by the prophets Elijah and Elisha may have been older or younger. (1 Kings 17: 20-23; 2 Kings 4:32-37) In view of these past resurrections of children, is it not right to expect that a large-scale resurrection of children will take place during Jesus' rule as king? Most assuredly! We can be certain that whatever

Jehovah God has purposed in this regard will be the just, wise and loving thing for all concerned.

The Bible reveals that by far the majority of mankind—men, women and children—will be raised from the dead. As the apostle Paul affirmed in his defense before King Agrippa: "I have hope toward God . . . that there is going to be a resurrection of both the righteous and the unrighteous." (Acts 24:15) The "righteous" are those who lived in God's favor. The "unrighteous" are the rest of mankind. But does that mean that every dead individual will have a resurrection? No, it does not.

### THOSE WHO WILL NOT BE RESURRECTED

Certain ones have been judged by God as undeserving of a resurrection. Regarding those who in the present time refuse to submit to Christ's rulership and fail to do good to his "brothers" on earth, the Bible says: "These will depart into everlasting cutting-off." (Matthew 25:46) They will experience this everlasting cutting-off when Jesus Christ, along with his angelic forces, destroys all opposers of his righteous rule in the "great tribulation," now near.

As to any in line for the kingdom of the heavens who prove unfaithful to God, we are told: "There is no longer any sacrifice for sins left, but there is a certain fearful expectation of judgment and there is a fiery jealousy that is going to consume those in opposition."—Hebrews 10:26, 27.

Also, there are classes of people who are spoken of as experiencing an eternal destruction. Jesus Christ indicated that the unrepentant Pharisees and other religious leaders of his day as a class had sinned against the holy spirit. He said of such sin: "Every sort of sin and blasphemy will be forgiven men, but the blasphemy against the spirit will not be forgiven. For example, whoever speaks a word against the Son of man, it will be forgiven him; but whoever speaks against the holy spirit, it will not be forgiven him, no, not in this system of things nor in that to come." (Matthew 12:31, 32) There being no forgiveness for such sin, all guilty of denying obvious manifestations of God's spirit pay the penalty for such unforgivable sin by remaining dead forever.

Aside from what the Bible says specifically about those who have perished everlastingly, we are in no position to say that particular individuals will not be raised from the dead. The fact that some will not be, however, should serve as a warning to us to avoid a course leading to divine disapproval.

## A RESURRECTION OF JUDGMENT

The fact that the majority of mankind will be raised from the dead is truly an undeserved kindness on God's part. It is something that God does not have to do, but his love and compassion for humankind moved him to lay the basis for it by providing his Son as a ransom. (John 3:16) That any humans would fail to appreciate their being raised from the dead with the prospect of eternal life is, therefore, hard to imagine. Yet there will be some who will not develop full, unbreakable, loyal attachment to Jehovah God. They will therefore lose out on the lasting blessings that being brought back to life will offer them.

Jesus Christ called attention to this when he spoke of a "resurrection of judgment" and set it in contrast with the "resurrection of life." (John 5:29) The fact that life is here contrasted with judgment makes it clear that a condemnatory judgment is involved. What is this condemnation?

To understand this, contrast first the situation of those resurrected to earthly life with that of those resurrected to heavenly life. The Bible says of those sharing in the "first resurrection": "Happy and holy is anyone having part in the first resurrection; over these the second death has no authority." (Revelation 20:6) Raised to immortal life in the heavens, the 144,000 joint heirs of Christ *cannot die.* Their loyalty to God is so certain that he can entrust them with an indestructible life. But this is not the case with all those raised to life on earth. There will be some of these latter ones who will become disloyal to God. The condemnatory judgment passed on them for unfaithfulness will be "second death," a death from the "authority" of which no recovery is possible.

Yet why would anyone end up following a course leading to condemnatory judgment when he has been granted the undeserved favor of being raised from the dead?

The answer to this question can be better understood in the light of what Jesus Christ said about people who would be resurrected. Addressing his unbelieving fellow countrymen, Jesus said:

"Men of Nineveh will rise up in the judgment with this generation and will condemn it; because they repented at what Jonah preached, but, look! some-

thing more than Jonah is here. The queen of the
south will be raised up in the judgment with this
generation and will condemn it; because she came
from the ends of the earth to hear the wisdom of
Solomon, but, look! something more than Solomon is
here."—Matthew 12:41, 42; Luke 11:31, 32.

With reference to a city that would stubbornly
refuse to listen to the message of truth, Jesus
noted:

"It will be more endurable for the land of Sodom
and Gomorrah on Judgment Day than for that city."
—Matthew 10:15; see also Matthew 11:21-24.

How would it be more endurable on Judgment
Day for Sodom and Gomorrah? How would the
"queen of the south" and the Ninevites who
responded to Jonah's preaching condemn the
generation of Jesus' fellow countrymen?

This will be in the way such resurrected ones
respond to the help given during the reign of
Jesus Christ and his 144,000 associate king-
priests. That period of rulership will be a "Judgment Day" in that it will provide all persons
opportunity to demonstrate whether they want
to submit to God's arrangements. In the case of
those like the unbelieving inhabitants of cities
who witnessed the powerful works of Jesus
Christ, this is not going to be easy.

It is going to be hard for them to recognize
humbly that they were wrong in rejecting Jesus
as the Messiah and then to have to submit themselves to him as their King. Pride and stubborn-
ness will make submission more difficult for them
than for the inhabitants of Sodom and Gomorrah,
who, while sinful, never rejected grand opportunities like those set before persons who witnessed
the works of Jesus Christ. The better response

of the resurrected Ninevites and that of the queen of Sheba will serve as a reproof to the resurrected generation of Jesus' fellow country-men living in the time of his earthly ministry. It will be much easier for these Ninevites and similar ones to accept the rule of someone toward whom they had never been prejudiced.

Those who positively refuse to make progress in the way of righteousness under Christ's king-dom will experience the condemnatory judgment of "second death." In certain cases this will happen before they reach human perfection.

Furthermore, others, after having been brought to human perfection, will unappreciatively fail to demonstrate loyal devotion to Jehovah God when put to the test. Following the thousand-year reign of Christ, Satan the Devil will be released for a short time from his confinement in the abyss. As he attacked God's sovereignty to seduce Eve, who then persuaded Adam, he will again seek to get perfect humans to rebel against God's rulership. Of Satan's attempt and its outcome, Revelation 20:7-10, 14, 15 says:

"As soon as the thousand years have been ended, Satan will be let loose out of his prison, and he will go out to mislead those nations in the four corners of the earth, Gog and Magog, to gather them together for the war. The number of these is as the sand of the sea. And they advanced over the breadth of the earth and en-circled the camp of the holy ones and the beloved city. But fire came down out of heaven and de-voured them. And the Devil who was misleading them was hurled into the lake of fire and sulphur . . . This means the second death, the lake of fire. Furthermore, whoever was not found written in the book of life was hurled into the lake of fire." This signifies their unending destruction or annihilation. Thus these unfaithful ones will have what Jesus called "a resurrection of judgment," a condemnatory judgment.

On the other hand, those who refuse to join Satan in rebellion will be judged worthy of receiving everlasting life. They will forever rejoice in having life as perfect humans, expressing love and being loved for all eternity. Theirs will prove to be a "resurrection of life."

Even now we can start to develop the qualities that God looks for in those whom he recognizes as his approved servants. If we show ourselves appreciative for all that he has done and get an advance start in the way of righteousness, we can have the wonderful prospect of having far more than the present life. Yes, we can have life everlasting in perfection, free from all sorrow and pain!

## CHAPTER 21

# How Can You Have More than This Life?

FROM all the foregoing information it is abundantly clear that there is much, much more to life than what we now experience. Just think of it—Jehovah God has set before mankind the grand prospect of life here on earth under righteous conditions, with freedom from sickness and death! It can be yours to enjoy, not just for a hundred years or a thousand years, but forever.

And the time when this will become reality is so near at hand!

Will you be among those to benefit from the realization of God's glorious purpose for man and his home, the earth? You definitely can be. But you need to act without delay. We are now living at the time when the Bible's warning takes on great urgency: "Before there comes upon you people the burning anger of Jehovah, before there comes upon you the day of Jehovah's anger, seek Jehovah, all you meek ones of the earth, who have practiced His own judicial decision. Seek righteousness, seek meekness. Probably you may be concealed in the day of Jehovah's anger." —Zephaniah 2:2, 3.

The "burning anger of Jehovah" is against all who have misled their fellowmen by lying about God and his purpose. And he does not hold guiltless those who support such men by attending their religious services or being members of their organizations. The time left before the execution of divine judgment is short. If you are a lover of righteousness you need to act quickly to obey the Scriptural command to break all ties with the world empire of false religion. Take seriously the urging of God's Word, which says: "Get out of her, my people, if you do not want to share with her in her sins, and if you do not want to receive part of her plagues." —Revelation 18:4.

But it is not enough simply to break off one's connections with organizations that have tolerated and encouraged unrighteousness. The Bible puts us on notice that God's "wrath is being revealed from heaven against all ungodliness and unrighteousness," yes, against the practices themselves

and those who continue to indulge in them.
(Romans 1:18) It does not leave us in any
doubt as to what those practices are. It clearly
identifies them and urges all who would have
Jehovah's approval to clean such things out of
their lives. Love for Jehovah and gratitude for
his goodness can make such a change possible.
—Ephesians 4:25–5:6; Colossians 3:5, 6.

This is no time to seek to justify oneself, pre-
suming that the good deeds that one does from
day to day more than offset one's shortcomings.
Setting their own standards of good and bad led
to calamity in the case of Adam and Eve. And
even in our day the Bible proverb is true that
says: "There exists a way that is upright before
a man, but the ways of death are the end of it
afterward." (Proverbs 16:25) Now is the time,
then, to learn Jehovah's ways, to seek his "righteousness." This is also the time to "seek meekness," that is, to be submissive to God's judgment
and humbly to accept his correction and dis-
cipline, conforming to his will. Only by doing this
will it be possible for you to be "concealed in
the day of Jehovah's anger."

Do not conclude, as some have, that your way
of life has been too bad for God to forgive you.
Rather, take comfort from the words addressed
to unfaithful Israelites of old: "Let the wicked
man leave his way, and the harmful man his
thoughts; and let him return to Jehovah, who
will have mercy upon him, and to our God, for
he will forgive in a large way." (Isaiah 55:7)
Also, find encouragement in his promise that
says: "Though the sins of you people should prove
to be as scarlet, they will be made white just like
snow; though they should be red like crimson

cloth, they will become even like wool."—Isaiah 1:18.

Jehovah God has no pleasure in executing judgment against anyone but wants all to enjoy life. (2 Peter 3:9) Still, Jehovah cannot and will not condone unrighteousness. Hence, it is necessary for all who would have his approval to repent of their former way of life and to change their ways to conform to his righteous will.—Isaiah 55:6.

The thing to do now is to start to learn what God requires of you, to take in the vital knowledge contained in his Word, and then to act in harmony with it. This is the way that leads to eternal life. (John 17:3) Jehovah's Christian witnesses will gladly give you personal help in acquiring an accurate knowledge of the Bible, free of charge. They also welcome you to their Kingdom Halls, where they regularly discuss God's Word.

## A TRULY BENEFICIAL WAY

By responding to the things you learn from the Bible, you will experience beneficial changes in your life. You will find that the application of Bible principles will improve relationships at home, at work and in your daily contacts with fellowmen. (Romans 12:17-21; 13:8-10; Ephesians 5:22–6:4; 1 Peter 3:1-7) This will contribute much toward making your life happier, more contented and meaningful even now.

Of course, this does not mean that you will be immune from the problems and pressures of the world. You are still going to be living among people who have no love of righteousness, and some of them will no doubt endeavor to discourage you from learning and applying the

Bible in your life. (2 Timothy 3:12; 1 Peter 4:4) But, as you grow in knowledge of God's Word, you will find that you are able to cope with the problems of life far more effectively than do those who rely on mere human reasoning. Instead of becoming bitter because of injustices that you may suffer, you will know the reason for them and will have the firm conviction that God's kingdom by Christ will soon put an end to all these things that detract from full enjoyment of life.—2 Peter 3:11-13.

As you acquire faith in God's loving provisions for eternal life, you will gain freedom from the oppressive influence that the prospect of death has had on all mankind. No longer will the falsehoods that have been taught concerning death mar your enjoyment of life. The shortsighted view that this life is all there is will lose any influence that it may have had toward tempting you to sacrifice right principles and a good conscience in an effort to get ahead in the world. The conviction that God can and will bring the dead back to life will enable you to gain freedom from the fear of death itself. Faith based on an accurate knowledge of God's Word will make it possible for you to enjoy life now as never before and to rejoice in the grand prospect of the future—everlasting life in God's righteous new order.

May appreciation for the loving provisions that God has made for mankind kindle in you a burning desire to know and to do his will. May it move you, with a sincere heart, to join with the psalmist who said: "Make me know your own ways, O Jehovah; teach me your own paths. Make me walk in your truth and teach me, for you are my God of salvation."—Psalm 25:4, 5.

# THE FUTURE FOR MANKIND
## Is Connected with Its Past

◆ Is man's past connected with mindless evolution and thus governed by chance? If it is, what future does humanity have? On the other hand, if man originally was created by God, then the purpose of God determines what the future holds for mankind.

But what about the evidence that scientists give on behalf of evolution? This is discussed in the thoroughly documented 192-page book **Did Man Get Here by Evolution or by Creation?** Examine that evidence and see for yourself which is most reasonable—a popular theory or the Bible's account of man's origin and his future.

DID MAN GET HERE
BY EVOLUTION
OR BY CREATION?

◆ But how can a person be sure that the Bible truly is from God? Read the 192-page book **Is the Bible Really the Word of God?**

To obtain either of these attractive hardbound books postpaid, just send 25c, or 50c for both.

Write to **Watchtower**, using an address from the next page.

# WHAT WAS FORETOLD ABOUT OUR DAY AND THE FUTURE

Events foretold by the Bible for our day have come to pass. This gives you a basis for strong confidence in what the Holy Scriptures say about the future. Did you know that the Bible foretells a thousand years of peace? Would you like to have thrilling details about this thousand-year reign of Jesus Christ? Do you want a preview of the blessings it will bring? Then obtain and read the book **God's Kingdom of a Thousand Years Has Approached.**

This volume also discusses the amazing events foretold for our day, as found in the Bible at Matthew chapters twenty-four and twenty-five. Explained are Jesus Christ's prophetic parables of the ten virgins, the talents, and the sheep and goats. How they relate to your future is made clear. This hard-covered 416-page book will be sent to you postpaid for just 50c.

If you would like to have someone visit your home to discuss Bible questions with you, write to **Watchtower** at an address given below.

---

ALASKA 99507: 2552 East 48th Ave., Anchorage. AUSTRALIA: 11 Beresford Road, Strathfield, N.S.W. 2135. BAHAMAS: Box N-1247, Nassau, N.P. BARBADOS, W.I.: Fontabelle Rd., Bridgetown. BELIZE: Box 257, Belize City. BRAZIL: Rue Guaíra, 216, Bosque da Saúde, 04142 São Paulo, SP. CANADA: 150 Bridgeland Ave., Toronto, Ont. M6A 1Z5. CONGO REPUBLIC: B.P. 2.114, Brazzaville. ENGLAND: Watch Tower House, The Ridgeway, London NW7 1RN. FIJI: Box 23, Suva. FRANCE: 81 rue du Point-du-Jour, 92100 Boulogne-Billancourt. GERMANY (WESTERN): Postfach 13025, 62 Wiesbaden-Dotzheim. GHANA: Box 760, Accra. GUYANA: 50 Brickdam, Georgetown 16. HAWAII 96814: 1228 Pensacola St., Honolulu. HONG KONG: 312 Prince Edward Rd., Second Floor, Kowloon. INDIA: South Avenue, Santa Cruz, Bombay 400054. INDONESIA: Jl Batuceper 47, Jakarta Pusat, DKI. IRELAND: 86 Lindsay Rd., Glasnevin, Dublin 9. JAMAICA, W.I.: 41 Trafalgar Rd., Kingston 10. KENYA: Box 47788, Nairobi. LEEWARD ISLANDS, W.I.: Box 119, St. Johns, Antigua. LIBERIA: P.O. Box 171, Monrovia. MALAYSIA: 20 Scotland Close, Penang. NEWFOUNDLAND, CANADA A1C 2M1: 239 Pennywell Rd., St. John's. NEW ZEALAND: 6-A Western Springs Rd., Auckland 3. NIGERIA: P.O. Box 194, Yaba, Lagos State. PAKISTAN: 8-E Habibullah Rd., Lahore 3. PANAMA: Apartado 1386, Panama 1. PAPUA NEW GUINEA: Box 113, Port Moresby. PHILIPPINE REPUBLIC: 186 Roosevelt Ave., San Francisco del Monte, Quezon City D-503. RHODESIA: P.O. Box 1462, Salisbury. SIERRA LEONE: Box 136, Freetown. SOUTH AFRICA: Private Bag 2, P.O. Elandsfontein 1406. SRI LANKA, REP. OF: 62 Layard's Road, Colombo 5. SWITZERLAND: Ulmenweg 45, P.O. Box 477, CH-3601 Thun. TRINIDAD, W.I.: 2 La Seiva Road, Maraval, Port of Spain. UNITED STATES OF AMERICA: 117 Adams St., Brooklyn, N.Y. 11201.